WORDS AND POETRY

WORDS AND POETRY

BY

GEORGE H. W. RYLANDS, M.A.

FELLOW OF KING'S COLLEGE, CAMBRIDGE

WITH AN INTRODUCTION BY

LYTTON STRACHEY

"Every line has been produced by me with labor pangs."—*Letter of Coleridge.*

". . . what we call the magic of words—thereby pleasantly avoiding the necessity of thinking out what we really mean."—LASCELLES ABERCROMBIE.

PAYSON & CLARKE LTD.
New York
1928

Printed in Great Britain by R. & R. CLARK, LIMITED, *Edinburgh.*

TO

MY FATHER AND MOTHER

AUTHOR'S NOTE

IN PRINTING my Fellowship dissertation I have not attempted to convert the enthusiasms of an undergraduate into the *ex cathedra* instruction of a don, but as the impartial editor of a former self have but revised a little, excised a little. As I cannot recapture the state of feeling in which the first part was conceived and composed, it would be dishonest and discordant to insert arguments, suppress sentiment or glose over immaturities in the light of later experience. The second part—a more specialised and detailed study, in which some of the principles of the first part are applied —contains more recent work. It has occupied me up to the present and will continue to do so, as such a study must ever be infinite, teeming, bountiful as mines of India.

G. H. W. R.

September 1924–*July* 1927.

CONTENTS

PART I

PART II

INTRODUCTION

A STORY IS TOLD of DEGAS, who, in the intervals of painting, amused himself by writing sonnets, and on one occasion found that his inspiration had run dry. In his distress, he went to his friend Mallarmé. " I cannot understand it," he said; "my poem won't come out, and yet I am full of excellent ideas." " My dear Degas," was Mallarmé's reply, " poetry is not written with ideas; it is written with words."

Mr. George Rylands' book is a commentary on Mallarmé's dictum. Was it a platitude? Was it a paradox? Both and neither, perhaps, like most profound observations; and Mr. Rylands explains to us how this may be—explains with the delicate amplitude of sensitive enthusiasm and the fresh learning of youth.

It is pleasant to follow him, as he explains and explores. The wide rich fields of English literature lie open before us—the paths are flowery—the nosegays many and sweet. We are lured down fascinating avenues of surmises; we ask questions, and all is made clear by some cunningly chosen bunch that is put into our hands, full of unexpected fragrances, or, perhaps, by the moon. We begin to understand why it is that the glory of an April day cannot be fickle and must be uncertain; we realise the difference between hills and mountains; to our surprise we detect a connection between Dr. Johnson and the Shropshire Lad. With such a clever guide, we may well at last grow presumptuous and long to do a little exploring on our own account.

But it is not an easy business. Perhaps of all the creations of man language is the most astonishing. Those small articulated sounds, that seem so simple and so definite, turn out, the more one examines them, to be the receptacles of subtle mystery and the dispensers of unanticipated power. Each one of them, as we look, shoots up into

> A palm with winged imagination in it
> And roots that stretch even beneath the grave.

It is really a case of Frankenstein and his monster. These things that we have made are as alive as we are, and we have become their slaves. Words are like coins (a dozen metaphors show it), and in nothing more so than in this—that the verbal currency we have so ingeniously contrived has outrun our calculations, and become an enigma and a matter for endless controversy. We say something; but we can never be quite certain what it is that we have said. In a single written sentence a hundred elusive meanings obscurely palpitate. With Mr. Rylands' help we analyse the rainbow; we dissect and compare and define; but the ultimate solution escapes us; we are entranced by an inexplicable beauty—an intangible loveliness more enduring than ourselves.

The value of a word depends in part upon the obscure influences of popular expression and in part upon the fiat of poets and masters of prose. A great artist can invest a common word with a miraculous significance—can suddenly turn a halfpenny into a five-pound note. He can do more: he can bring back a word that has been dead for centuries into the life and usage of every day. What now passes as a Bradbury was once—before the poet touched it with his muttered abracadabra—a rusty bit of metal in a collector's cabinet. The romantic writers of the early nineteenth century were the great masters of this particular enchantment; and it is owing to them that to-day a multitude of words and phrases go familiarly among us, which, no less familiar to the Elizabethans, were unknown and unintelligible even to the learned men of the age of Pope and Gray.

But neither can the poets themselves escape the thraldom of their own strange handiwork. They, too, are the slaves as well as the masters of words. Even the greatest of them all, perhaps! There is one name that no English writer on English literature can hope, or wish, to avoid for more than a very few moments together. Before we are aware of it, we all of us find that we are talking about Shakespeare. And Mr. Rylands is no exception. Naturally, inevitably, he devotes the latter half of his book to a consideration of Shakespeare as a user of words, and to the history—

the romance, one might almost say——of his adventures
among them.

It is curious that Shakespeare——by far the greatest
word-master who ever lived——should have been so
rarely treated of from this point of view. We know
almost nothing of the facts of his life; we can only
conjecture, most hazardously, about his opinions and
his emotions; but there, fixed and palpable before us,
lie the vast accumulations of his words, like geological
strata, with all their wealth of information laid bare to
the eye of the patient and curious observer. How very
remarkable, for instance, is the development, which
Mr. Rylands points out to us,——a late and unexpected
development——in Shakespeare's use of prose! How
extremely interesting is the story of his dealings with
words of classical derivation! The early youthful
engouement for a romance vocabulary, the more mature
severity, and the recoil towards Saxon influences, and
then the sudden return to a premeditated and violent
classicism——the splendid latinistic passion which,
though it grew fainter with time, left such ineffaceable
traces on all his later life!

A drama might almost be made of it——and a drama
that could hardly have passed unconsciously in
Shakespeare's mind. The supreme artist must have
known well enough what was happening among those
innumerable little creatures who did his bidding with
so rare a felicity——his words. Did he, perhaps, for
his own amusement, write an account of the whole
affair? A series of sonnets . . . ? If an allegory
must be found in those baffling documents, why should

not this be the solution of it?   One can fancy that the beautiful youth was merely a literary expression for the classical vocabulary, while the dark lady personified the Saxon one.   Their relations, naturally enough, were strained, yet intimate. . . .   The theory is offered gratis to the next commentator on the Sonnets. There have been many more far-fetched.

Shakespeare, certainly, knew what he was doing; and yet, in the end, he found that those little creatures were too much for him.   So it appears: the geological strata put it almost beyond a doubt.   The supreme word-master lorded it no less over character and drama; for many years he carried those three capacities together in an incredible combination, pushing them on from glory to glory; until something most un-expected happened: the words asserted themselves, and triumphed, with extraordinary results.   In Shake-speare's later works character has grown unindividual and unreal; drama has become conventional or operatic; the words remain more tremendously, more exquisitely, more thrillingly alive than ever—the excuse and the explanation of the rest.   The little creatures had absolutely fascinated their master; he had become their slave.   At their bidding he turned Coriolanus from a human being into a glorious gramophone; they spoke, and a fantastic confusion, a beautiful impossibility, involved the constructions of *The Winter's Tale* and *Cymbeline*.   To please them, he called up out of nothingness, in *The Tempest*, an Island, not of Romance, but of Pure Style.   At last, it was simply for style that Shakespeare lived; everything else had vanished. He began as a poet, and as a poet he ended. Human beings, life, fate, reality—he cared for such things no longer. They were figments —mere ideas; and poetry is not written with ideas; it is written with words.

LYTTON STRACHEY.

PART I

I

POETRY AND PROSE. DIFFERENCES OF APPEAL

Of little use the man you may suppose
Who says in verse what others say in prose.—POPE.

I

WE STILL HANKER AFTER a definition which will
draw a dividing line between poetry and prose;
we still endeavour to distil the essence of poetic pleasure
into a neatly labelled crystal phial. Confident that
" we know poetry when we see it ", we can invent no
formula for the label. Pope and Crabbe have won the
title of poet no less than Chaucer and Keats, and the
acceptance of the Book of Job and Walt Whitman, of
the Song of Solomon and Sacheverell Sitwell, removes
further boundaries. Is it then a step or a gulf that lies
between these last and, say, the purple passages of
Walter Pater or the perorations of Sir Thomas Browne?

There are certain main sources of difference
between poetry and prose to be kept in mind; difference of function and appeal, difference arising from
literary tradition and convention, and difference of
practical technique. In this chapter I shall consider
the first two questions, and, by adumbrating my own
general theories and noting some popular but significant errors and beliefs, attempt to clear the air for
the discussion of word-values, ornament and style in
poetry, which is the purpose of this book.

Prose, roughly speaking, is employed for the clear statement of facts, for various forms of rhetoric and for the study of character. In each case metre and rhyme will be a handicap, making excessive demands upon the ingenuity of the writer, who, whatever artifices he may use, is careful, as a rule, to disguise them and appear natural. The scientific writer abhors ornament; his facts must speak for themselves; they have only to be collated and arranged to the best possible advantage. His words have meaning, but no visual, vocal or emotional values. He does not, like the historian, give his " sense of fact ", for the historian is in part a scientific, and in part an imaginative writer (or novelist) in a proportion which varies according to his intellect, conscience and disposition. The orator differs from the poet in that he is more concerned with exciting other men's emotions than expressing his own. He will not be ashamed to deceive, and, since he speaks with a purpose, since he has to move his audience on behalf of something which they have less at heart than he, will overstate and fake his own emotions. At one moment he will counterfeit spontaneity and extempore speech, at another he will flaunt crude rhythms and extravagant language, relying on voice and gesture to carry them off. His excess will not be fine, because his effect must be immediate. Dramatic poetry oscillates between poetry and rhetoric and combines the methods of both. To be fully relished the Greek and the Elizabethan tragedies must be both read and seen on the stage. Poetry becomes rhetoric when the playwright sacrifices the truth of the emotions experienced

by his characters to the reaction in his audience.
When Zanche, the Moor, cries:

> I am proud
> Death cannot alter my complexion,
> For I shall ne'er look pale,

and Edward II.:

> Tell Isabel the queen I looked not thus,
> When for her sake I ran at tilt in France
> And there unhorsed the Duke of Claremont,

the scales are evenly balanced. Both passages demand the voice and are, to some extent, conscious and
rhetorical. The simplicity of the diction, and the
prose order of words are largely responsible for their success and natural effect. Restoration tragedy provides
many contrasts, as, for example :

> Then will I smear these walls with blood, disfigure
> And dash my face, and rive my clotted hair,
> Break on the flinty floor my throbbing breast
> And grovel with gashed hands to scratch a grave,
> Stripping my nails to tear the pavement up
> And bury me alive. . . .
>
> *The Mourning Bride.*

This is not a study of hysteria: it signifies a jaded
audience. " Where there is leisure for fiction, there
is little grief."

Modern poets have poached upon the preserves of
prose, and modern novelists are returning the compliment. Their reprisals are justified. In the elaborate
processes of character-creation poetry has its function.
Action, dialogue and the analysis of sensations and
motives are the flesh, blood and bone of which the

creatures of fiction are born and bred, but the " atmosphere" which they breathe, and the background before which they move, are often suggested best by the *poetic* expression of *poetic* experience. This is the case in the novels of Conrad, of Stella Benson, of D. H. Lawrence, of Virginia Woolf :[1] it is the case in *The Cherry Orchard*, of all plays the one nearest akin to the novel: poetry and realism alternate and heighten one another. Novelists are learning the secret from the drama. Euripides, Shakespeare and Ibsen were all masters of this device. As regards these moments of poetic prose, we may quote Tchekov's dictum on style: " Cut out all those pages on the moonlight and give us what you really feel—the reflection in a piece of broken bottle ". Whether that advice produced a rhymed stanza, *vers libre* or a prose paragraph, we should to-day call it poetry.

In only one then of these three chief functions of prose has poetry a part, and that a small one. Her functions and methods of appeal, her traditions and conventions, her subjects and style, are peculiar to herself. They have been created, changed and coloured by conditions, in part natural, in part arbitrary. In the early days of any civilisation, when few

---

[1] Novelists (with the exception of Arnold Bennett and the old school) are abandoning descriptive detail. They no longer " number the streaks of the tulip ". They describe emotionally, impressionistically like the poet. In *Mrs. Dalloway* the striking of Big Ben inspires a rhythmical phrase which is repeated throughout the novel like a refrain—

> " First a warning, musical,
> Then the hour, irrevocable,
> The leaden circles dissolved in the air."

can read or write, the muse is a maid of all work. She has to entertain and to instruct, to hand down the deeds, real or imaginary, of gods and heroes, and to fit words to musical modes and the stamp of feet, on secular and religious occasions. Metre begins by being the essential characteristic, the skeleton of poetry, and ends by becoming an ornament, as artificial as the instinct that gave birth to it is natural. Poetry is older than prose, because of the assistance metre gives to the memory, before the time of printed books, and because in the salad days of literature, the more rules there are, the easier it is to write; when we are still in the nursery we use double lines and a copy-book. Relieved by prose of her more arduous duties, poetry began to develop more and more grand ideas, and to pride herself on being very sophisticated and well-bred. Now a democratic age has come and prose is threatening revolution.

II

It is not my purpose here to follow the stream of poetry from Greece to Italy, from Italy to France, and thence to England. The pioneers in English poetry poured new wine into old bottles with surprising success. Chaucer, Wyatt and Surrey, the Elizabethan singers and sonneteers, imitated extremely artificial foreign models. In fact, they had excellent copy-books and learnt the tricks of the trade without tears. For them the gulf between poetry and prose was already a wide one. They inherited certain conventions and modified them to fit their own taste and talent. During the last three hundred years, new fashions, new social conditions, new influences from the past and from abroad, have altered and enlarged the possibilities of poetry still further.

The original link that bound poetry and song was a strong one, but after the Restoration it rusted away. The troubadour had passed from the earth; the serenade, as man's standard of comfort became higher and his self-consciousness more acute, yielded to the English climate. Above all, the hand of the courtier had lost its cunning; he could no longer perform upon the lute. Instead he occupied himself with translating the Odes of Horace. The decay of song was not regrettable. Poetry was to find more scope in the development of the ode and the revival of the ballad. Music and poetry were not very compatible except in infancy. Their "school-days' friendship", like that of Helena and Hermia

> sitting on one cushion,
> Both warbling of one song, both in one key,

turned to rivalry. Either the words or the notes have to take second place. A Campion, a Moore, may occasionally effect a compromise and create not one work of art but two—on the printed page and on the lips of the singer. But "Full fathom five" loses by being sung, in the same way as *Lear* loses by being performed.

The love-song attained all the variety and perfection of which it is capable in the era which begins with Wyatt and closes with Milton, and then languished. The tradition, or truth, that flourished long

before the Middle Ages and the Courts of Love, before
Petrarch and Chaucer's young squire, before the
bastard Faulconbridge jeered at the Dauphin, namely
that love is the subject of lyric poetry and that all
young lovers attempt a " woeful ballad to their mistress'
eyebrow ", flourishes still. And although at the
present time the psychologist and the psychological
novelist have monopolised the subject, some years will
pass before the lover tears his hair in the composition,
not of love verses, but of a page of Proust. The
reason is not hard to find, it is twofold. In the first
place, the convention is strong that to write verse is
thereby to license any extravagancy of the tongue, the
imagination and the desires. Secondly, by repeating
the current and familiar phrases, symbols and ideas of
poetry, by conjuring the moon, by naming the nightingale and the rose, or comparing the beloved to Helen
of Troy, the lover finds relief exactly as an angry man
does by swearing. In both cases certain words have
acquired curious emotional values. There are, of
course, other minor points: for instance, that the scale
is small and finite and suitable to the expression of a
single and simple idea, that there are rules to cling to,
and that for the inarticulate, old tags and quotations
serve as a word-and-phrase book in a strange country.

Poets have another duty. They tell us what we
have been told in our cradle, and have afterwards
learnt from bitter experience. Man demands a philosophy of life, however irrational and paradoxical: he
believes that there is a rainstorm because he has forgotten his umbrella. He likes poetry to repeat familiar

lessons, more or less metaphorically disguised, and to read in Horace, Herrick and A. E. Housman that life is short and youth is shorter.   In the Greek tragedies and in Shakespeare, in Spenser, Wordsworth and Pope, such γνῶμαι abound.[1]   At one time this gave rise to the belief that poetry should instruct.   *The Defence of Poetry* utters it for the last time, in the tone not of a schoolmaster but of the idealist, and there is a faint echo in the criticism of Matthew Arnold.   These γνῶμαι appeal to the middle - aged as erotic poetry appeals to the young.   Life brings to each man the same elementary and fundamental conclusions that it has brought to his forefathers, and meeting the truisms in the poets, where they are neatly and feelingly isolated, he has all the pleasures of " recognition ", of saying—" It is so and I have found it so ".   The limitations of poetical technique invite epigrammatic expression.

As I have said, the appeals of poetry are largely determined by social conditions, and it is therefore not unnatural that in this modern world of advertisement and noise, where works of art are few and far between, and, in the case of pictures, imprisoned in dark rooms, poetry is looked upon as offering a refuge from life.   One person opens the Oxford Book and repeats a perfectly familiar poem, another steps out of

[1] " Thence what the lofty grave Tragedians taught
In chorus or iambic, teachers best
Of moral prudence, with delight received,
In brief sententious precepts while they treat
Of fate and chance and change in human life."
MILTON, *Paradise Regained*.

the crowded street into the cool gloom of Westminster Abbey and repeats a perfectly familiar prayer. Ever since the Romantic Revival, the poetry of romantic escape, as it is called, has become more and more popular. The poets themselves fled from " the weariness, the fever and the fret ". Wordsworth is an obvious example.[1] Sensitive and excitable, moody and egotistical, he hated London and Londoners and buried himself in the Lake District, sacrificing inspiration to tranquillity. Even William Morris, who did not stop his ears to the hum of the world, became, as a poet, absorbed in the Middle Ages and the lulling monotonies of mediaeval verse. Meanwhile, from afar were heard the voices of industry and science prophesying war. Very foolishly the poets hid their heads deeper in the sand. They conjured up castles in the air and recalled the golden ages of the past: they became infinitely remote and poetical, until at last the eighteen-nineties caused an explosion of laughter. The pageant faded, the bubbles burst, and the muse was, to say the least, discredited. Future poets will take the advice of Mr. Haldane and bow down before the gods of the Philistines. There is no such thing, cry the new school, as an unpoetical subject; and they have the Elizabethans on their side. Poetry, as Professor Grierson has shown, has a wide background and draws inspiration from many springs of knowledge; but Arnold's complaint that " the poets of the

---

[1] And Shelley—

" The ebb and flow of the world vexes me, I desire to be left in peace."—
Cancelled passage of Preface to " Adonais."

first quarter of the century did not *know* enough "
breaks down with Shelley, who dabbled in chemistry
and became a disciple of Godwin, with Coleridge who
sacrificed poetry to philosophy as much as to opium.
The telescope and the circulation of the blood may have
inspired good poetry, but will not, therefore, make a
poet. Our complaint is, not that the poets did not
know enough, but that they turned away from the world
about them, that they did not face human activities and
relationships and attain a philosophy of life from the
study of mankind, in man and in themselves; that
much of the best of Keats is in his letters and not in
Shakespearian sonnets.

When Christianity tottered, further demands were
made upon the poets—demands which they could
satisfy without hypocrisy. They had always been
prepared to link up the spirit of man with the
manœuvres of the planets. Blank ignorance of the ways
of God and the meaning of the universe gives free
scope for magnificent conjecture; and we swallow the
poetical sublime without straining at the gnat of
mysticism. Whether or not we " think the heavens
respond to what we feel ", the invocations of Ajax and
Prometheus, Lear asking the heavens to pity him,
because they themselves are old, Romeo shaking the
yoke of inauspicious stars from his world-wearied flesh,
and Vaughan's vision of eternity are no whit less over-
powering. Poets are welcome to play oracle. " To
make the sun, the stars and the moon guilty of our
disasters is ", as the bastard Edmund remarks (very
properly in prose), " the excellent foppery of the

world ", but the atheist in moments of acute physical and mental pain cries out " My God! ", and if the poet wishes to hear the music of the spheres or to see the moon with a star in its nether tip, the still, small voice of common sense is silent.[1]

Poetry should be simple, sensuous and impassioned; and that quality of sensuousness satisfies appetencies in an educated person not unlike those of the typist who reads *Three Weeks* and frequents the cinema. Luxury is no unusual day-dream. The Renaissance led poetry prisoner in a red-rose chain. The Song of Solomon, the translations of Ronsard and the pseudo-Anacreon combined to inspire the erotic beauty of Marlowe's *Hero and Leander*, the little prettinesses of the canzonets of Lodge, and the religious ecstasies of the Fletchers and Crashaw. The roses withered round the marble porticoes and stucco pillars of the eighteenth century, only to blossom with a more wild and natural grace in Keats, Rossetti and Swinburne. These in their turn gave way to more rare and unnatural blooms, as the quality of sensuousness grew less simple, less impassioned, and more exquisitely neurotic.

I have touched lightly enough upon some of the

[1] Arnold puts the whole matter with clarity and truth: " The grand power of poetry is its interpretative power; by which I mean not a power of drawing out in black and white an explanation of the universe but the power of so dealing with things as to awaken in us a wonderfully full, new and intimate sense of them, and of our relations with them. When this sense is awakened in us, as to objects without us, we feel ourselves to be in contact with the essential nature of those objects, to be no longer bewildered and oppressed by them, but to have their secret and to be in harmony with them; *and this feeling calms and satisfies us as no other can.*"

popular pleasures and appeals of poetry, and implied that the last five and a half centuries have curiously confused and combined in its character the natural, the conventional and the sophisticated. It is time now to attempt a summary, if not a definition.

The poet is an artist and words are his medium. He endeavours to re-create the feeling with which any important experience, actual or imaginary, has possessed him; a feeling of joy, perhaps, or reverence, or passionate love, of indignation or scorn, of fear or pity or regret. And the re-creation of that state of feeling enables him also to express the knowledge and truth, whether old or new, which has been the fruit of his emotional experience.

As the Greek tragedians set their audience at the winning post, so the poet starts his flight from a higher emotional plane than the writer of prose. The historian, the novelist, the orator begin in a low key; they reserve their strength. Space and time are theirs, space in which to accumulate detail, in which to persuade and convince, time even to tease and baffle and keep us in suspense. The poet scarcely allows us to poke the fire or settle a cushion at our back. He startles us with a question or command and then takes wing.

> Go and catch a falling star.
>
> Shall I compare thee to a summer's day?
>
> O what can ail thee, knight at arms?

It is as if we were sitting for a portrait and had been snapped by a photographer. The poet knows the exact pitch of his climax. He may give us the climax, the vision alone, or the downward flight, the reaction, or, as in *La Belle Dame Sans Merci, The Highland Reaper* and *Woodspurge*, the whole experience. The advantage of being able to start in whatever key he pleases is both caused by, and compensates for, the smaller compass of his instrument. His second advantage is that he is the favourite of language. If his words are numbered, yet the whole past of poetry has coloured them with associations and endowed them with peculiar values. And these are the values in which he trades; he has not to explain but to move and suggest. And the very fact that the words are limited, their dependence upon the length of the line, the rhythms of the stanza, the pattern of the poem, isolates and increases their powers and opens the way to the manipulation of delicate inter-verbal harmonies and contrasts of sound and sense. Poetry has in consequence been much employed for purpose of experiment in style and technique; for the invention of complicated metrical and rhymed systems, and the use of ornament for ornament's sake. This has, of course, given further support to the " plain man's " complaint that poetry is essentially artificial and unreal.

The poetic instrument is a delicate one, its technical compass is small. The poet is content to play a familiar tune upon our emotions. He expresses " the general passions, thoughts and feelings of men "; he aims his shaft at the heel of Achilles. He knows the weaknesses of human nature and gratifies desires in us

which other people satisfy in religion, perhaps, or the
cinema, in eating caviare,[1] or saying " I told you so ".
He shifts, varies and reconciles his moments of appeal;
of appeal to the head and heart, the eye and ear, the
memory, the senses, the imagination. A poem is a
harmonised series of these moments, each one perfect
in itself and intrinsically valuable. To put it differently, it is not so much what poetry says that matters,
as her remarkable way of saying it. She must give
eternal expression to eternal truths.

To-day, however, she is treated with scant respect.
The novel, thanks perhaps to Flaubert's perpetual
martyrdom in search of the *mot propre*, to Anatole
France with his eight sets of proofs and ruthless nail-
scissors, has become a reputable occupation, if not an
art. Jane Austen, who complained so bitterly of the
supercilious reader, can rest in peace. But the prestige
of poetry has suffered.

If the novelist seeks the *mot propre*, how much more
so the poet. His words are isolated, arranged in a
metrical pattern, where not only the value, or values,
of each single word must be considered, but also the
close interdependence of one upon the other: for every
word is quick to take colour from its companion, and
will gain or lose in emphasis according to its position
in the line. The adjustment is very delicate, the
labour painful. A lyric by Wordsworth dances gaily
enough: yet that stolid figure would first pace for

---

[1] Harebrain in *A Mad World, My Masters*, describes the *Hero and
Leander* and *Venus and Adonis* as " two luscious marrow-bone pies for a
young married wife ".

many days up and down the back garden, "humming and booing about", and scattering scraps of paper as he went.

Is it more polite, or more intelligent, to call the poet a wizard? Even Mr. Strachey, who tilts an eyebrow at sentiment, is ready to endow the poet with a magic wand. But since we all of us chatter and scribble, devour books and newspapers and advertisements, give ear to preachers and cheap-jacks, have all of us suffered from the man who flogs a dead epithet, have all enjoyed an epigram and essayed a peroration, it behoves us to possess some first-hand knowledge of the scientific and emotional values of words: we must be able to analyse the meaning and appeal of the few score that make up our favourite sonnet.

Professor Saintsbury, in a paper on Shakespeare and the Grand Style, praises the line

> The uncertain glory of an April day,

and remarks that to substitute *fickle* for *uncertain*, or *splendour* for *glory*, is, for no apparent reason, to destroy the poetry. But there is a reason, and the critic should lay his finger on it. What are the associations of the word *glory*? "Ichabod, Ichabod, the glory has departed." *Sic transit gloria mundi.* There is a natural link, an interdependence between *glory* and *uncertain*. Splendour suggests the glare of summer, not the sunshine of spring. Shakespeare has *glory* in another similar context:

> A brittle glory shineth in his face;
> As brittle as the glory is the face.

C

And Shirley:

> The glories of our blood and state
> Are shadows not substantial things.

Further, the Bible and Prayer Book have enhanced the emotional value of the word.   Then, why not *fickle*? First because it has no associative link with *glory*, secondly because it makes the line too light and careless: the three long syllables of *uncertain* and the elision give weight and seriousness to the line.   Thirdly, the word *fickle* brings in different feminine associations and tends to turn April into the girlish creature of William Watson's lyric.   And it is " the spring of love ", in the context, not the beloved, which is represented as uncertain (and not as faithless).

Why, to take another instance, was the first line of *Endymion* so much better after Keats' alteration?

> A thing of beauty is a constant joy

expresses one thought;

> A thing of beauty is a joy for ever

expresses two.   An adjective is never above suspicion. *Never* and *for ever* are highly emotional in poetry; they bring in the sense of Time:

> For ever and for ever farewell, Brutus.
>
> Quoth the Raven, Nevermore.

Transience and eternity have man's heart and head at their mercy.   Time is an infallible poetic subject.

Again, the famous line in *The Tempest*:

> The fringéd curtains of thine eye advance,

which has thrown critics into controversy and into raptures, has only been half examined. In *Pericles* we have—" Her eyelids . . . begin to part their fringes of bright gold "; it is even more decorative. But surely the peculiar poetic character of Prospero's line (and this critics have missed), which distinguishes it from the words of Pericles, lies largely in the word " advance "? Take two other instances: one from *Romeo and Juliet*:

> Beauty's ensign yet
> Is crimson in thy lips and in thy cheeks,
> And death's pale flag is not *advancèd* there;

and one from an anonymous Elizabethan lyric:

> I saw my Lady weep
> And sorrow proud to be *advancèd* so.

Prospero's line is a piece of *poetic diction*: advance— unfamiliar, with a certain military pomp about it— heightens the effect and takes us by surprise, like Hamlet's

> Absent thee from felicity.

It is in perfect harmony with the elaborate imagery or conceit, a conceit which is quite justifiable, for the eyes, in Shakespeare, are very often called "windows".

Words, then, their meanings and implications and emotional values, are the subject of the following chapters. For this, I believe, is the only possible way in which to approach the question—What is Poetry? Yet no critic to my knowledge has employed the microscope. Whether our pleasure is increased by seeing how the wheels go round, is, ultimately, a matter

of opinion.   There are who deny that criticism can be
of any service in the true appreciation of creative work.
To examine, they say, is to destroy.   But poetry is not,
like religion, dependent upon faith, and critical analysis,
like tragedy, has a peculiar pleasure of its own.   Evil
days come and the years draw near when we cease to
experience the same thrill of high excitement and wild
surmise, and no new poets swim into our ken.   Middle
age has its mitigations, and in those days let us not
despise the perdurable, if second-best fascination of
criticism, but substitute for the joys of motion the
understanding of mechanics.   Besides, how does the
bliss of ignorance compare with the subtleties of
experience, or the delight of surprise with that of
expectation?   Were oysters more captivating upon the
first than upon the thousandth occasion?   Would
Valmont of *Les Liaisons Dangereuses*, past master of
seduction and intrigue, be ready to change places with
the hero of Booth Tarkington's *Seventeen*, or the school-
boy in *Limbo*, suffering erotic nausea for the first time?
Has not every Romeo had his Rosaline?   Fortified by
these oratorical questions we can proceed to pull our
toy to pieces to see how it works.

STYLE AND DICTION

If poetry comes not as naturally as the leaves of a tree, it had better not come at all.—KEATS' *Letters*.

If blank verse be not tumid and gorgeous, it is crippled prose.—Dr. JOHNSON.

MOST CRITICS AND ESSAYISTS who take the one word " Style " for their title, curiously confine themselves to various forms of prose. If poetry is their subject, they head the page " The Grand Style ", " The Sublime ", or " Poetic Diction ". Coleridge gave as a working definition of prose " the right words in the right order ", and of poetry " the best words in the best order ". Are we then to conclude that prose is the milk of literature and poetry the cream, the one nourishing and essential, the other a luxury enjoyed in smaller quantities? But then Arnold goes so far as to say that Wordsworth has no style. Where, one asks, is Style to be found if not in poetry; where in poetry, if not in Wordsworth?

We will make the popular view our starting-point. It centres round the question of ornament. Poetry, it is felt, is always in court dress, setting out for the ball in feathers and diamonds, " sails filled and streamers waving ". But if we analyse the appeal of certain single lines of especial intensity, we find that the reverse is true. Take for example:

> O God, O God, that it were possible
> To undo things done.
> HEYWOOD.

Since there's no help, come let us kiss and part.
DRAYTON.

For God's sake, hold your tongue and let me love.
DONNE.

Christ, that my love were in my arms,
And I in my bed again.
Anonymous.

But she is in her grave, and oh,
The difference to me!
WORDSWORTH.

Thou'll break my heart, thou bonnie bird,
That sings upon the bough;
Thou minds me o' the happy days
When my fause luve was true.
BURNS.

There is economy here; the words are those of daily life, the syntax is simple and straightforward. The effect is that of naked speech heightened by emotion. Metre lays the right emphases and makes the words more interdependent, more inevitable. When metre attempts the realism of broken utterance, as in the dying speeches of Ford, the result is curiously feeble.

At certain moments, then, the poet strips his verse of all ornament, he seeks the natural, not the startling word. These moments are prepared for and led up to; they rise like mountain peaks above wooded slopes; they are apices which demand a bareness of style intolerable for any length of time. If we turn to fiction we shall find similar moments of climax, marked by a few words of dialogue or the conclusive comment of the author. " There comes a moment—' I will dance with you ', says Emma—which rises higher than the rest, which though not eloquent in itself or violent, or

made striking by beauty of language, has the whole
weight of the book behind it." In poetry, when such
a moment comes, when Lear cries:

> She'll come no more,
> Never, never, never, never, never.

or Vittoria Corombona—

> My soul, like to a ship in a black storm,
> Is driven, I know not whither.

the words have not only the whole play behind them,
but the whole of what we call "Life", that is, the
knowledge which is the fruit of literature, of history,
and of our own individual experience. Lyric no less
than dramatic poetry achieves these moments. In
La Belle Dame Sans Merci, in *The Highland Reaper*, no
word is too "poetical", too rich in suggestion and
association, until the imagination is beguiled, the
emotions excited, and at last the forcible simplicity of
the climax, "not eloquent in itself or violent", speaks
out:

> Will no one tell me what she sings?

> And I awoke and found me here
> On the cold hillside.

The more intense the emotion, the more the poet will
abhor ornament: he will counterfeit direct speech.

This "elemental" simplicity is quite distinct from
that of the balladist who has a story to tell, distinct also
from the childlike simplicity of the first Pre-Raphaelites; and Morris and Rossetti are often story-tellers in
verse. "Elemental" simplicity: the words recall the
famous Preface to the Lyrical Ballads. This is perhaps

the best opportunity for a brief record of the truths and the fallacies to which the Wordsworth-Coleridge controversy gave birth. The dust has long since settled, the essential passages of the text are familiar enough. With Sir Walter Raleigh as a guide, there is no need to linger long.

The chief fallacies of the Preface are exploded in the *Biographia Literaria*. Coleridge points out that the best parts of language are the products, not of clowns and shepherds, but of philosophers: that the language of metrical composition is essentially different from that of prose: that Wordsworth at his best breaks his own rules, and even when he observes the prose choice of words, does not observe the prose order. Wordsworth and Coleridge are right and are at one in their condemnation of the false diction of the Ned Softlys of the coffee-house, a diction which Milton created to no small extent, and of which not only Thomson and Cowper but also Wordsworth himself, particularly in *The Evening Walk*, provide striking examples. But Coleridge mistook in proposing the " neutral " style of " the mob of gentlemen who wrote with ease ", as Wordsworth's true model. It was not to the classical poets of England and France, to Malherbe, Jonson and Pope, that he wished to prove his allegiance. The phrases in the Preface, " a selection of language really used by men ", " the essential passions of the heart ", " our elementary feelings ", " a plainer and more emphatic language ", foreshadow aims and aspirations in poetry far more profound than those of Waller or Suckling or even the "well-languaged" Daniel whom, as Coleridge observes, he sometimes resembles.

Let us consider for a moment the doubts and ideas of another poet in a parallel position. *Love's Labour's Lost* is, as it were, the preface to Shakespeare's work. In it we see him facing the literary fashion of the day, as Wordsworth was to face the conventions and clichés of the eighteenth century. Berowne mocks the affected extravagance of Armado and rails at honey-tongued Boyet, yet he himself is not free of the "delicate foppery of language", as Pater calls it. When a crisis comes in his love and his emotions are engaged, he shakes it from him.

> Taffeta phrases, silken terms precise,
>   Three-pil'd hyperboles, spruce affectation,
> Figures pedantical; these summer flies
>   Have blown me full of maggot ostentation:
> I do foreswear them; and I here protest,
>   By this white glove—how white the hand, God knows,—
> Henceforth my wooing mind shall be expressed
>   In russet yeas and honest kersey noes.

In Berowne Shakespeare seems to analyse himself. The *Venus and Adonis* had been composed in the artificial manner of the day: it was to yield to the "plainer and more emphatic language" of the Sonnets which deal with the "essential passions of the heart". To a young poet Euphuism had its temptations. A Shakespeare or a Keats would be attracted by its undoubted qualities of delicacy, fitness and even beauty. The fashions against which Wordsworth reacted had no such charm. And even so they would not have appealed to his stubborn and turbulent nature. Indeed, Wordsworth's taste led him in exactly the opposite direction to euphuism, away from the dainty and fantastic, the extravagant and the ornate. For him the barest fact in the briefest word was, as Professor Raleigh has said, poetry in essence. " The dates on a tombstone spoke eloquently; and a parish register, without addition, touched the springs of sympathy and tears."

The aims and aspirations at the back of the Preface to the Lyrical Ballads are excellent enough, but Wordsworth was not the man to put them into words. " He suffered himself to express in terms at once too large and too exclusive, his predilection for a style the most remote possible from the false and showy splendour which he wished to explode. It is possible that the predilection, at first merely comparative, deviated for a time into direct partiality." Such is the cool verdict of Coleridge who had raised the same banner of rebellion.

Simplicity is the key-note of three styles in poetry. In one style the simplicity is passionate and direct, the simplicity of one who must speak out. Here, if anywhere, art is the " removal of surplusage ". The meaning of the words, a message, a question, a command, an entreaty, a cry, whatever it may be, is all that matters. The effect of metre is subdued, a subconscious stimulant and a means of making the phrase complete. At moments of intense feeling, when repetition, particularly rhythmical repetition, is not uncommon, poetry and prose join hands, as in Cornelia's speech, which follows blank verse and precedes a prose passage.

> O you abuse me, you abuse me, you abuse me,
> How many have gone away thus for lack of tendance.
> Rear up's head, rear up's head; his bleeding inward will kill him.

But it is in the Elizabethan drama that we shall find the functions and styles of prose and poetry most nearly interchangeable. They are fused into stage speech, a live, easy, hybrid form. On the one hand the stresses of the decasyllable had been endlessly varied and shifted, the syllables themselves endlessly resolved, the realistic possibilities of enjambment and parenthesis fully mastered; on the other, blank verse had rung in the ears of these actor-dramatists like a popular music-hall tune from their youth up, drowning the other harmony of prose.[1] We do not find such confusion again until *Leaves of Grass* and the poems of Gertrude Stein at the present time.

I quoted at the beginning of this chapter from *A Woman Killed with Kindness*, and it is not irrelevant here to note Lamb's remarks on Heywood's style. " He is a sort of prose Shakespeare. His scenes are to the full as natural and affecting. But we miss the poet, that which in Shakespeare always appears out and above the surface of nature." The truth is that this elemental simplicity is not for continual use in poetry but, as we have seen, for sudden moments, when the prose order of words will tell most strikingly. A

---

[1] Mr. Dobree in *Histriophone* gives good examples of the interchangeable poetry and prose movement of the later Elizabethan dramatists.

single sonnet may succeed in this style, like Shake-speare's

> Being your slave, what should I do but tend
> Upon the hours and times of your desire ;

but Heywood employs it for too long at a stretch.   A great poet varies his style and thus increases the tension.

The second simplicity, that of the " neutral " style, is artificial, the simplicity of neatness.   Nature occasionally breaks through and changes the simplicity into that of the first kind, as in Carew's

> Now you have freely given me leave to love,
>   What will you do?

but as a rule the prose order is not observed and the tricks and delights of metre and rhyme are carefully studied.   Ben Jonson introduced the light classical manner and the Cavalier and Restoration lyrists followed him, although they were not seldom beguiled by the metaphysical conceits of Donne.   We shall find this same simplicity, in which the meaning of every word counts and metre counts more, in the couplets of Pope.   The style is not formed for emotional expression, but for a finished and final recordation of familiar truths and γνῶμαι, of a witty suggestion or remark. Examples are numerous.

> The grave's a fine and private place,
> But none, I think, do there embrace.
>   MARVELL.

> Too full already is the grave
> Of fellows that were good and brave
> And died because they were.
>   HOUSMAN.

Underneath this stone doth lie
As much Beauty as could die:
Which in life did harbour give
To more Virtue than doth live.
                                JONSON.

Our very hopes belied our fears,
Our fears our hopes belied—
We thought her dying when she slept,
And sleeping when she died.
                                HOOD.

'Tis better to have loved and lost
Than never to have loved at all.
                                TENNYSON.

Leave such to trifle with more grace and ease
Whom Folly pleases, and whose Follies please.
                                POPE.

Brevity is the soul of wit and metre a grace and reason thereunto. In Suckling, Prior and Pope, the masters of this style, verbal ornament is rare. A more classical poet, an Andrew Marvell or an A. E. Housman, does not confine himself to one single style.

The simplicity of the third style is not so much that of language as of thought. It does not arise from intensity or from neatness. If there is ornament, it is not far-fetched and distracting. Thus in *The Blessed Damozel* the imagery is concrete, the detail pictorial and immediately visualised. Her yellow hair is compared to ripe corn, the earth to a fretful midge, the moon to a little feather. The vision is made real by the complete simplicity of—

Until her bosom must have made
The bar she leaned on warm.

" The most unimaginative man ", says Macaulay,
" must understand the *Iliad*. Homer gives him no
choice and requires of him no exertion." The
similes and metaphors are, indeed, easily compre-
hended and to the point. This Homeric simplicity is
to be found in the ballads, in Chaucer, in the *Defence
of Guenevere*, in the *Bride's Prelude*. In the ballads
we have simplicity of two kinds, that of—

> The youngest stood upon a stone
> The eldest came and pushed her in;

and

> She has taken her little pen-knife
> And twinned the sweet babes of their life,

which is childlike and without art; and also the
simplicity of—

> And what will ye leave to your ain mither dear,
> Edward, Edward?
> And what will ye leave to your ain mither dear,
> My dear son, now tell me, O?
> The curse of hell frae me sall ye bear,
> Mither, mither;
> The curse of hell frae me sall ye bear,
> Sic counsels ye gave to me, O!

which is elemental.

The best contrast of the two kinds is instanced by
comparing the work of Chaucer and Sir Thomas Wyatt.
Chaucer has high seriousness perhaps, but not intensity; as a story-teller he has not even the intensity
of the ballads. When the crisis in *Troilus and Criseyde*
comes, he stammers pitifully and lets it pass; there is
no psychological tragedy:

> For she so sory was for her untruth,
> Y-wis, I wolde excuse her yit for ruth.

Cressida was " a daughter of the game " as Shakespeare knew, as Wyatt would have known. Where faithlessness is the subject, the latter speaks out.

> Such hammers work within my head
> As sound nought else into my ears.

There is no better account of the elemental simplicity of poetry than this. Wyatt and Wordsworth had that quality in common. The sophisticated simplicity of a Sedley is unknown to them.

The degrees and gradations of the ornamental style in poetry (or rather of all styles which cannot be called simple), elude definition and classification. They range from the natural detail of John Clare, the pretty conceits of the Elizabethan song-books, the felicities of Tennyson, the audacities of Donne, to Milton's jewelled mosaics, Spenser's gentle redundancies, and the squandered inheritance of Swinburne and Keats. There are, in fact, as many ornamental styles as there are poets; it is from the ornament that we shall know the man. The simple style tends towards the impersonal. If, for a short time, the orbits of poetry and prose seemed to be drawing together, from now on we shall find them widely divergent.

The prose writer is distinguished from the poet, in that he travels far and never loses sight of his destination. His purpose is to progress, his way is the highway. Lamb objected to *Peter Bell*, because the narrative is slow; whereat Crabb Robinson observed with some acuteness, ". . . to object to the poet a want of progress is as absurd as to object to the dancer that he does not get on.   In both alike the object is to give delight by not getting on." The analogy is just: but a poem in so far as it is of the narrative or dramatic kind should advance, just as the waltzer should circle the ball-room. Poetry differs from prose in the same respect as ballet dancing differs from a hurdle race or a walking tour, although the three latter are all forms of physical exercise. On the question of progress depends the importance of ornament. How should we react in a page of prose to such phrases as " Time's winged chariot ", " The opening eyelids of the morn ", " Youth's sweet-scented manuscript ", " The fringéd curtains of thine eye "? They would be obstructive, out of place, idle as a pirouette on a tarred road. They are amplifications, justified in poetry by their intrinsic beauty; whereas the felicities of prose contribute to the meaning of the whole and are wheels in the machine. Let us contrast " in the dark backward and abysm of time " with " the Areopagy and dark tribunal of our hearts ". Sir Thomas Browne is an exotic writer; his mind and his material demanded more scope and freer rhythms than poetry allows, but his language is undeniably poetical. Nevertheless, he does not use ornament for ornament's sake. He does not set his foot on the primrose path of peri- phrasis. His vocabulary is large, literary, individual; he experiments with words, delighting to combine native and foreign elements. In " the Areopagy and dark tribunal of our hearts" the *meaning*, not as in Prospero's phrase, the *suggestiveness*, of every word tells. His phrases are condensations, not amplifications. If Milton's names are texts for a stanza, Browne's phrases are texts for a sermon or essay. The ornament in good prose is functional; in poetry it is calligraphic. Keats writes " the morn was clouded but no shower fell "; that is the walking step of the dancer. Wait a moment.

> Though in her lids hung the sweet tears of May.

He twirls: a familiar flourish handed down from the Book of Job to Marlowe, Middleton and Milton, " the eyelids of the morn ". The first line tells us all we need to know; a prose writer by now is round the corner and out of sight. The poet beautifies. His devices are employed not to make us see but to make us feel, not to inform but to delight. They are calligraphic. " I look upon fine phrases as a lover ", wrote Keats; and it expresses exactly the poetic point of view, the passionate but *objective* feeling for ornament. Browne's phrases well up from his prolific fancy, they are not pursued and netted like bright butterflies. Milton has an interesting confession in his *Vacation Exercise*:

> I have some naked thoughts that rove about
> And loudly knock to have their passage out,
> And weary of their place do only stay,
> Till thou has decked them in their best array.

It is objective in tone and curious after his condemnation of the " new-fangled toys and trimmings slight " and " the late fantastics ". The Metaphysical poets expressed elaborate conceits in simple language; Milton provided his naked thoughts with classical liveries and a mythological wardrobe.

D

We may digress for a moment here to note that ornament in poetry is to no small extent controlled and
directed by metrical considerations.   In the modern
Irish play *Juno and the Paycock*, disaster and death fall
upon a woman who has struggled for years to keep her
squalid home together: her husband is a drunkard, her
daughter is deserted and finally her son is shot.   Then
her nature gives way in a terrible cry to the Virgin:

Where were ye, Mother of God, when they riddled him with
bullets, when they riddled him with bullets; O God, take away our
hearts of stone and give us hearts of flesh.

Others besides myself remembering the words may
have put beside them this appeal:

> Where were ye, nymphs, when the remorseless deep
> Closed o'er the head of your loved Lycidas;
> For neither were ye playing on the steep
> Where your old bards the famous Druids lie,
> Nor on the shaggy top of Mona high,
> Nor yet where Deva winds her wizard stream.

The two passages give one an insight into the different
functions and aims of poetry and of tragic prose.   The
second is an escape, a purgation of suffering by beauty
of sound and distraction of thought.   But the elaborate
decoration of *Lycidas* is, of course, demanded by the
metre and the scale of the poem.   Our pastoral elegies,
Astrophel, *Adonais*, *Thyrsis*, Gray's *Elegy*, the funeral odes
of Bridges and the rest, are built up of stanzas or
paragraphs, and in all of them the instrument employed is the decasyllable, varied here and there with
a half line.   There must be a current flowing from
stanza to stanza, and each stanza must have an internal

movement of its own. The stature of the whole requires and can set off the richest ornaments. Like the Greek tragedian, it wears the buskin and the mask; its " gestures " are conventional and few. The true English elegies on the other hand are lyric. They are based on the six-syllabled or, better, the eight-syllabled line; there the diction is as restrained and as economical as prose can be; for example in the epitaphs of Jonson and the dirges of the Elizabethan drama, in King's *Exequy*, in *Rose Aylmer*, in the Lucy poems, in parts of *In Memoriam*.

The ornament of prose consists in detail, in numbering the streaks of the tulip, in delicate and accurate observation. Such detail in Wordsworth is a fatal blemish. In Clare it is more pleasing because it is not an ornament, but his very subject. The short-sighted Tennyson is a master craftsman and alchemist. He condenses his observation into an epithet, and employs descriptive detail at selected moments with economy and restraint. Even so his eye is of small value compared with his ear.

The similes of Milton, Keats and Matthew Arnold are elaborated and pursued until the original point of comparison is lost. They are not functional. They have two values. Their similitude or significance in the context is not visual but emotional: for example:

> Those green-rob'd senators of mighty woods,
> Tall oaks.   *Hyperion*.

> faint-smiling like a star
> Through autumn mists.
> *Endymion*.

or the comparison of Rustum and his dying son to the eagle crying for his mate:

> never more
> Shall the lake glass her flying over it;
> Never the black and dripping precipices
> Echo her stormy scream as she sails by.

The second value, closely bound up with the first, is that they are delightful or intriguing in themselves, their cause and context being momentarily forgotten. In the first book of *Paradise Lost*, Satan is compared to that Sea-Beast,

> *Leviathan*, which God of all his works
> Created hugest, that swim th' Ocean stream:
> Him haply slumbering on the *Norway* foam
> The Pilot of some small night-foundered Skiff,
> Deeming some Island, oft, as Seamen tell,
> With fixed Anchor in his skaly rind
> Moors by his side under the Lee, while Night
> Invests the Sea, and wished Morn delays;

and his shield to the Moon, whose Orb

> Through Optic Glass the *Tuscan* Artist views
> At Ev'ning from the top of *Fesole*,
> Or in *Valdarno*, to descry new Lands,
> Rivers or Mountains in her spotty Globe.

The diver in pearly seas in *Hyperion*, the drudge and the worker in Pekin, in *Sohrab and Rustum*, provide other examples; but the most notable of all is without doubt that of the Grecian coaster intruding on the Tyrian trader's ancient home, which is the subject of the two last stanzas of *The Scholar Gipsy*.

Two further points may be remarked when contrasting the uses of ornament in prose and poetry. Where do we look for purple in a prose writer? In the peroration; in the more heightened and excited passages. " The proper time for using metaphors ", says Longinus, " is when the passions roll like a torrent and sweep a multitude of them down in resistless flood. For it is the nature of passions in their vehement rush to sweep and thrust everything before them, or rather to demand hazardous turns as altogether indispensable." He is speaking of oratory, but the words apply in the main to all prose. With poetry the very reverse takes place. Poets " apparel the *least* phrase they speak ". Where prose puts on his panoply, poetry goes unarmed. Their methods of warfare are as different as those of David and Goliath. Shakespeare's tragedies perhaps offer some exceptions, but in poetic drama rhetoric has a part and his style is exceptional, bursting with metaphors and instances, despite himself. Even so Hamlet, Lear and Othello are often most simple when most terrible, and the final cry of Troilus is—

> O Cressid, O false Cressid! False, false, false!
> Let all untruths stand by thy stained name,
> And they'll seem glorious.

The second point of difference is that whereas prose preserves a regular and even style, whether coloured and poetic as in Jeremy Taylor, or athletic and direct as in Dryden, from the beginning to the end, poetry varies her methods and her pace from stanza to stanza, from line to line. Sometimes the sound, sometimes the symbol is the thing: conceits and

metaphors alternate with naked thinking simplicity.
The effect of this is to heighten and isolate phrases, to
throw a searching beam upon the words. So much
for the general use of ornament in poetry as contrasted
with prose; we have now to examine the use of words
more closely.

Metre has certain effects upon language. First of
all it creates boundaries and limits, which are very
useful. The poet may override them, when he so
desires: but even in the blank verse of, say, Shirley,
there remains the visual division, and the actor pauses
imperceptibly at the end of the line. One advantage
of these boundaries is that they enable the changes of
style, noticed above, changes which are unnatural and
almost impossible from sentence to sentence in prose.
Housman's *Last Poems* will give an example of a
division, intensifying the language by contrast:

> The fairies break their dances,
>   And leave the printed lawn,
> And up from India glances
>   The silver sail of dawn.
>
> The candles burn their sockets,
>   The blinds let through the day,
> The young man feels his pockets
>   And wonders what's to pay.

The Italian sonnet form with the break between the
octave and sestet often occasions similar effects, and the
final clinching couplet of the Shakespearian sonnet,
not to mention Pope's exploitation of the heroic couplet,
show the possibilities of metrical boundaries.

Then again in a line which is separated off, a line

in which the words are numbered and must be fitted
as the figures are fitted into a pediment, it is possible to
achieve a harmony and interdependence of words, too
subtle for the ear to catch or the mind to grasp in the
swifter and more continuous reading of prose. The
invisible fetters with which the poet binds his words
together may be alliterative. Let us take another of
the *Last Poems*:

	On acres of the seeded grasses	s ss s
b n	The changing burnish heaves;	ch sh s
m m n	Or marshalled under moons of harvest	sh s st
n	Stand still all night the sheaves;	st st t sh
b n w	Or beeches strip in storms for winter	ch st st t
n w	And stain the wind with leaves.	st s

The play is mainly upon *sh ch st*. If it is objected
that Housman is an exceptionally careful artist, one
need only refer the unbeliever to an article by Stevenson
in the *Contemporary Review* (1885), analysing a passage
in *Troilus and Cressida*,[1] as follows:

But in the wind and tempest of her frown,	w p v f st ow
Distinction with a loud and powerful fan,	w p f st ow l
Puffing at all, winnows the light away;	w p f l
And what hath mass and matter by itself	w f h m
Lies rich in virtue and unmingled.	v l m

Verrall, as I have heard, used to point out Shakespeare's
artfulness in the rhetorical tricks of Brutus.

Who is here so *b*ase that would be a *b*ondman? If any, speak; for
him have I offended. Who is here so *r*ude that would not be a *R*oman?
If any, speak; for him have I offended. Who is here so *vi*le that will
not *lov*e his country? If any, speak; for him have I offended.

---

[1] Or to George Wyndham's analysis of the assonances and alliterations
in the first of Shakespeare's sonnets.

The blunt alliterations are followed by the inversion of *love* and *vile*. The art of poetry, according to a modern poet, consists in knowing exactly how to manipulate the letter S. The best example of this that I know is to be found in *Comus*.

th d t	A *thousand* fan*t*a*si*es	s s s
b th t	*B*egin *to th*rong in*to* my memory	
b d d	Of calling *sh*apes an*d b*eck'ning *sh*a*d*ows *d*ire,	sh s sh s
d t th b	An*d* airy *t*ongue*s that sy*lla*b*le men'*s* name*s*	s s s s
d d t d	On *S*an*ds*, an*d Sh*oars, an*d D*eser*t* Wil*d*er*ness*es.	s s sh sss

The Ss gather in number but are leavened with hard letters: L, M and N play a part also. The last line has two strong pauses which draw out the eight S sounds like a wind whistling over waste spaces.

Sometimes one letter appears and reappears, threading a poem or paragraph. Thus the less common letter V in Marvell's *Coy Mistress*. The first suggestion comes in three consecutive lines: *conversion*, *vegetable*, *vaster*; then *deserve*; then in the centre panel a combination with F. *Before*, *vast*, *found*, *vault*; *preserved virginity*; *grave*, *fine*, *private*. This panel of twelve lines is, indeed, subtle and faultless. The sixth line runs on and carries one over from the first into the second half: the beginning and the close are marked by a strong couplet. The second and fourth couplets have unstressed rhymes which keep up the speed.

Tennyson is a gentle juggler with words. He experiments with syllables:

> Myriads of rivulets hurrying through the lawn,

with letters:

> Between the loud stream and the trembling stars,

(Here the consonants repeat and the vowels are varied,
a common effect; the caesura is strong and the monosyllable *stream* robs *and* of its natural stress.)
with emphases:

> Coldly thy rosy shadows bathe me, cold
> Are all thy lights, and cold my wrinkled feet.

This last device, epanaphora, is frequent in Tennyson
and not rare in Milton. Metre enables the poet to
underline a word as it were: all shades of emphasis are
possible. Contrast, for instance, on the word *dear*:

> My dear and only love, I pray.
> > MONTROSE.
>
> I could not love thee, Dear, so much.
> > LOVELACE.
>
> If yet I have not all thy love,
> Dear, I shall never have it all.
> > DONNE.
>
> A terrible childbed hast thou had, my dear.
> > SHAKESPEARE.

This last famous line brings us to another point.
The emphasis falls upon *terrible* and *my dear*; hence the
poignancy of effect. The words heighten each other.
This is one of the chief artifices of the poet. He plays
off words one against the other so as to raise their
values. In the Housman poem already quoted, the
candles and *pockets* of the second stanza are intensified
by the *fairies* and *silver sails of dawn*. Or take the
couplet of Poe:

> Up shadowy, long forgotten bowers
> Of sculptured ivy and stone flowers.

Not only is there something unexpected in the combination of stone and flowers, but the combination of *shadowy* and *long forgotten* with *sculptured* and *stone* is most striking, of the abstract with concrete, the emotional with the visual. The verbal contrasts of poetry are infinitely important. Much depends upon arrangement, upon the juxtaposition of monosyllable with polysyllable, of dentals with liquids, of native with foreign, of the homely with the far-fetched. The contrast or contradiction may be one of idea as in " Ladies dead and lovely knights ". The two epithets *dead* and *lovely* lie up against each other, as in

> The many men so beautiful
> And they all dead did lie.

There is a good syllable contrast in the line—

> With sudden adoration and blank awe,

and also in Hamlet's

> Absent thee from felicity awhile
> And in this harsh world draw thy breath in pain,

where the Latin element gives place to the native and the slow pace of the second line suits both the sense and the gasps of the dying prince.

The Elizabethan dramatists not only " place " single words with sensibility and skill, but whole lines and allusions have an ironic significance. Marlowe puts in the mouth of the damned Faustus the cry of the lover in his mistress' arms:

> O lente, lente, currite noctis equi!

as it were

> Ah God, Ah God, that day should be so soon!
>
> SWINBURNE, *Provençal Burden.*

And how immensely the Webster passage,

> Come, come, my lord, untie your folded thoughts
> And let them dangle loose as a bride's hair;
> Your sister's poisoned,

gains from the half-realised connection between *sister* and *bride*. The ornament is not irrelevant but ironical. It is as the wife of Brachiano that Isabella has made such a tragic appearance earlier in the play: " a bride's hair " strikes a sinister prelude to Isabella's death.

The Elizabethans are rich in metaphors and images and striking verbal contrasts. Shakespeare particularly uses the concrete word, the outward and visible sign:

> Even at the teat thou suck'dst thy tyranny.

> And silken dalliance in the wardrobe lies.

They found nothing common or unclean or unpoetical, and could write without self-consciousness. " We are the stars' tennis balls ", " A harlot is like Dunkirk, true to none ", " I do account this world but a dog kennel ", " There's but a dining time 'twixt us and our confusion."

> This flea is you and I, and this
> Our marriage bed, and marriage temple is.

Dr. Johnson called Shakespeare to account for the

meanness of his language. "Every man, however
profound or abstracted, perceives himself irresistibly
alienated by low terms: they who profess the most
zealous adherence to truth are forced to admit that she
owes part of her charms to her ornaments; and loses
much of her power over the soul when she appears
disgraced by a dress uncouth or ill-adjusted." Truth
like love goes naked; better that the dress be uncouth
than meretricious. He goes on to say that he cannot
" check his risibility " at the ministers of justice
" peeping through a blanket". Risibility, blanket;
the *parvenu* word spurns the peasant. Longinus has
noted the value of a word which grazes the edge of
vulgarity. When a man unpacks his heart with words,
he *will* fall cursing like a drab. But Johnson's own
practice goes far towards contradicting his precept.

> Loosen'd from the minor's tether,
>   Free to mortgage or to sell,
> Wild as wind and light as feather
>   Bid the sons of thrift farewell.
>
> Wealth, my lad, was made to wander,
>   Let it wander as it will;
> Call the jockey, call the pander,
>   Bid them come and take their fill.
>
> Should the guardian friend or mother
>   Tell the woes of wilful waste,
> Scorn their counsel, scorn their pother,
>   You can hang or drown at last.

What a curious anticipation this is of the *Shropshire
Lad* ! Johnson's strictures were justified thus far:

it is not the downright word, the russet yeas and kersey noes, that are to be avoided in poetry, but those which have particular and vulgar associations beyond the control of the reader.

No word is naturally and intrinsically meaner than another; our opinion therefore of words, as of other things arbitrarily and capriciously established, depends wholly upon accident and custom. Words which convey ideas of dignity in one age are banished from elegant writing and conversation in another, because they are in time debased by vulgar mouths and can no longer be heard without the involuntary recollection of unpleasing images.

To-day we are familiar enough with *blanket* in the Macbeth context, and probably read the passage without much thought, or perhaps the atmosphere is too strong for us; we have succumbed as to an anæsthetic. A knife, at any rate, does not necessarily suggest butchers or cooks, nor is *dun* " seldom heard but in the stable ". Milton and Tennyson employ it. Nevertheless the principle is in the main true. Wordsworth was induced to cut out " goings-on " from one of his poems, and although the revised version is inferior in idea, one feels that the advice was just. The associations are sexual and facetious, the word a colloquial coinage.

The Greeks had a large number of forms and usages which were licensed in poetry and unpermissible in prose. English has its poetic diction but on a smaller scale, consisting of archaisms in whose poetic value Spenser believed (and he has had many disciples), and of second-hand phrases from the classics. Of these last Coleridge's schoolmaster made such short work. "Harp? Lyre? Pen and ink you mean. Muse. boy, Muse? Your nurse's daughter. Pierian spring? Oh aye, the cloister pump, I suppose." This is as extreme on the one side as Johnson was on the other. Both the familiar and the unfamiliar word, the natural and the artificial, tell in their right place in poetry, and it is the happiness of poetry that she can combine both. Housman has, on the one hand, *chap*, *lad*, *dinner*, *cricket*, *liquor*, *silly*, *sweetheart*, *luggage*, *dressed to the nines*; and on the other, *thews*, *sain*, *handselled*, *flambeaux*, *timbal*, *limbec*, *marl*, *aftermath*, *frore*, *darnel*, *nadir*.

The commonplaces of poetic diction, *swains*, *hinds*, and the like, and the circumlocutions imitated from the classics are not necessarily prosaic. All depends upon the motive, upon whether they are employed to delight or as a disguise, from a sense of beauty or from a sense of shame. In *Comus* the poetic diction of a former faces that of a latter age. Imagery and symbolism give way to artificial imitations. But Milton's artifices are the diversions of a scholar. The " feathery dames " and " finny drove " are not unpleasing in their context; but the " tame, villatic fowl " of *Samson Agonistes* are pompous and absurd. This classico-miltonic device of dressing the commonplace in sceptred pall and buskins had an irresistible attraction for the eighteenth-century poets, who employed it indiscriminately. Wordsworth, although content to praise the stock-dove and celandine, is not free of τὸ παρατράγῳδον. He is sometimes self-conscious, and being, like Milton, deficient in humour, gets out of touch with his medium.

> If touched by him
> The inglorious football mounted to the pitch
> Of the Lark's flight—or shaped a rainbow curve
> Aloft, in prospect of the shouting field!
>
> The indefatigable fox had learned
> To dread his perseverance in the field.
>
> *The Excursion.*

The football will not reach the poetic empyrean on the wing of the lark.   Let it fly of itself:

> Twice a week the winter thorough
>   Here stood I to keep the goal:
> Football then was fighting sorrow
>   For the young man's soul;

and

> Is football playing
>   Along the river shore,
> With lads to chase the leather,
>   Now I stand up no more?
>
> Ay, the ball is flying,
>   The lads play heart and soul;
> The goal stands up, the keeper
>   Stands up to keep the goal.

When the poet deals with the stars, the sunrise and the spring, he may be as fanciful, artificial and idealistic as he pleases: but where the subject is everyday but poetically unfamiliar, he must face it fair and square and rely upon force and economy and contrast, not upon ornament.

Poets have verbal preferences of their own.   It is intriguing to note the peculiarities of their vocabulary and use Shakespeare as a touchstone.   The atmosphere

of eighteenth-century poetry springs mainly from a few
words, common in Milton and rare in the Elizabethans.
Wordsworth shows great fondness for *placid*, *genial*,
pellucid, *social*, *sylvan*, *vernal*, *verdant*—Latin epithets,
which are not to be found in Shakespeare; nor are the
lawns of Milton.   Shakespeare has *rustic* three times
and *rural* twice—both Wordsworthian favourites.
Warble is a curious and not entirely pleasing word;
it has taken a slightly humorous colour.   Milton has
it on every page and, consequently, it is frequent in
Wordsworth.   Shakespeare has it four times, twice
comically.   The couplet—

> You curious chanters of the wood,
> That warble forth Dame Nature's lays

suggests a much later author than Sir Henry Wotton.
Warble never possessed nor could possess the poetic
power of *sing*, despite its soft musical sound.   For
song and *singing* have a certain idealistic quality: the
simple and familiar word is, as often, more emotional
in poetry.   The letter S is valuable.

> The singing masons building roofs of gold.

> In solemn troops and sweet societies
> That sing and singing in their glory move.

> When I am dead, my dearest,
> Sing no sad songs for me.

Warble is artificial and only applicable to brooks and
birds, or to human beings in the technical sense of
plucking the string.[1]

[1] Milton uses it of Shakespeare, but with the idea of a bird, of the shepherd
in *Lycidas*, where it is pure diction; and Shakespeare of Hermia and Helena,
but fondly.

Other points characteristic of poetic diction of that time are the use of the epithet *purple* to mean *bright*, as in the Latin *purpureus*,

> Here Love his golden shafts employs, here lights
> His constant lamp, and waves his purple wings.
> MILTON.

> The bloom of young Desire and the purple light of Love.
> GRAY.

and a weakness for epithets coined from substantives, such as *elmy, dampy, bloomy, lawny, orby, sphery*. These are, excusably, found in Elizabethan epistolary poetry, whence Keats adopted them along with the enjambed couplet.

The true poetic diction is, however, of a different order. It consists of an emotional vocabulary or code, of symbols rich in association, of images consecrated and conventionalised until they become clichés, except when presented musically, or in an unexpected light, or with a backward glance at an old style. With these the next chapter deals.

III

SYMBOLISM, ASSOCIATION AND NOMENCLATURE

Hast thou then nought wiser to bring
Than worn-out songs of moon and rose?—DE LA MARE.

When I make a word do a lot of work like that, said Humpty Dumpty,
I always pay it extra.—*Alice in Wonderland*.

THE INDIFFERENT MOON silvers the pages of Sappho and Propertius, of Sidney and Milton, of Keats, Byron and Thomas Hardy. Likened to a curled feather, a dying lady, a silver coin, she shines upon " Sweeny and Mrs. Porter " as she shone upon Jessica and Lorenzo. What then is her poetic significance and value?

While the Moor is smothering Desdemona, cries of foul murder break in upon him; he turns away and mutters:

It is the very error of the moon;
She comes more near the earth than she was wont
And makes men mad.

Although the popular superstition may have lost its hold on us, these words have intense emotional power. The moon becomes as it were the President of the Immortals, the symbol of Fate. We shiver, as we do at " all simples that have virtue under the moon " or " slips of yew slivered in the moon's eclipse ". In fact, *in certain contexts* to name the moon is (primarily and apart from the particular allusion or application) to fill us with fear. Consider as another example, Cleopatra's lines in the death scene of Antony:

> the odds is gone,
> And there is nothing left remarkable
> Beneath the visiting moon.

The emotions are stirred, but terror is mingled with pity. Here the moon is a symbol not only of fate, but also of mutability. We find the same association more clearly in *King Lear*:

> We'll wear out
> In a walled prison, packs and sects of great ones
> That ebb and flow by the moon.

But in the former quotation the suggestion is concealed in the one word " visiting ".

These associations are, however, secondary. The more simple and elementary value of the moon is as something beautiful in itself, and therefore a poetic subject, and the general association is not with lunacy or witches or the fall of empires but with romance and love. The emotion aroused is not one of fear but of delight. In the fifth act of *The Merchant of Venice* the moon provides the stage lighting of love and carries with it no further suggestion or idea; this familiar usage is emotional. When the poet particularises, when Milton describes moonrise in Paradise, when Rossetti compares the moon to a curled feather, the case is altered; it no longer has the same general emotional significance; a more visual or pictorial quality takes its place. Byron gives us an excellent example of the simplest poetic usage.

We'll go no more a-roving
So late into the night,
Though the heart be still as loving
And the moon be still as bright.

We'll go no more a-roving
By the light of the moon.

Bright we shall find, when dealing with adjectives, to be the poetic word for young, beautiful and alive; and Byron suggests by juxtaposition a symbolical relation between the love of the heart and the light of the moon, with the further implication that the heart has lost its youth. But if we put the lines besides those quoted from Shakespeare, we realise that our emotion is one of pity rather than of fear.

W. B. Yeats in *Ideas of Good and Evil* has the following significant passage: " There are no lines with more melancholy beauty than those by Burns,

The wan moon is setting ayont the white wave,
And Time is setting with me, O!

and these lines are perfectly symbolical. Take from them the whiteness of the moon, the wave, whose relation to the setting of time is too subtle for the intellect, and you take from them their beauty. But when all are together, moon and wave and whiteness and the last melancholy cry, they evoke an emotion which can be evoked by no other arrangement of colours and sounds and forms. We may call this metaphorical writing, but it is better to call it symbolical writing. . . ."

It is not metaphorical writing. Landor is metaphorical when he writes (with the same thought as Burns):

> I warmed both hands before the fire of life,
> It sinks and I am ready to depart;

and he is less effective. Not only because he appeals for our approbation, not our pity, and proclaims in the market-place what Burns cries in secret and almost involuntarily: the magic is in the moon and her associations. There is a close affinity between the lines of Burns and those of Byron, but the symbolical relation is more emphasised in the former. As in *Antony and Cleopatra* mutability and change are suggested, with this addition, that " the white wave " has reference to the power of the moon, " pale governess of floods ", and thus gives a fatalistic impression. The epithet here is " white " instead of " bright "; and the emotional difference is easily realised. "White" implies cold and solitariness and sets the key of the second line and the last melancholy cry.

It is worth remarking that in Burns's couplet the emphasis, after several soft vowels, falls sharply on the i sound of Time.

> The wan moon is setting ayont the white wave,
> And Time is setting with me, O.

The Greek tragic cry is αἴαι.

The associations of the moon contradict each other in a paradoxical way which is the secret of these effects. She is at once the symbol of love and romance, and of inconstancy and loneliness ; of the waxing and

waning of empires, and of eternity; for she herself
abides.

> Yon rising moon that looks for us again—
> How oft hereafter will she wax and wane;
> How oft hereafter rising look for us
> Through this same garden—and for one in vain!

The idea which is expressed here is the same as that
which with more economy and secrecy moves us in
Byron and Burns.

Or take Hardy's poem:

> Close up the casement, draw the blind,
> Shut out that stealing moon,

where the moon is the symbol of lost youth and love
and of present loneliness. Yet the poet says but little
more than Sappho:

> Δέδυκε μὲν ἀ σελάνα
> καὶ Πληΐαδες, μέσαι δὲ
> νύκτες, παρὰ δ' ἔρχεθ' ὥρα,
> ἐγὼ δὲ μόνα καθεύδω.

Do not the words imply more than that it is the hour
of midnight—a symbolical relation between the Pleiads
and the setting moon and the mortal lying alone?

The moon, the nightingale and the rose, they are
in themselves poetic subjects, the seed of poetry.
They are passwords; the lover names them and he
finds relief. Nor are they staled by use, but, on the
contrary, grow richer in poetic significance, gathering
more associations to them, as they go, like a rolling
snowball. They carry the past with them. " No
one knows through what wild centuries roves back
the rose." Keats's nightingale was heard " in ancient

days by emperor and clown " and sang to Arnold by
the sweet, tranquil Thames as once in lone Daulis
and the high Cephisian vale. Hardy's stealing moon
shone of old through Cynthia's casement.

> Donec diversas praecurrens luna fenestras,
> Luna moraturis sedula luminibus,
> Compositos levibus radiis patefecit ocellos.

The first poet stands in the desert and whispers
" The moon "; the last, the most sophisticated, to
whom all words have become common and impure,
takes a sheet of vellum and writes

THE MOON.

Thus the whirligig of time brings in his revenges. For
the most elementary poetry lies, as Wordsworth thought,
in the mere names of natural objects. Good wine needs
no bush, the moon and the rose need no epithets and
similes.

The rose is perhaps too familiar a piece of poetic
stage property to be dwelt upon at length, but one must
not forget that the Elizabethans in whose pages roses
are " as common as blackberries " grafted a foreign
slip on to a wilder native stock. The word was
already coloured with heraldic and allegorical associations and possessed a religious significance.

> Of a rose, a lovely rose,
> Of a rose is al myn song.

> The flour sprong in heye Bedlem,
> That is bothe bryht and schen:
> The rose is Mary hevene qwyn,
> Out of here bosum the blosme sprong.

It is a convention in the ballads:

> He had a rose into his hand
> He gave it kisses three.

> He's killed the may and he's laid her by
> For to bear the red rose company.

The Renaissance rose is the hothouse variety, with French petals and an Alexandrine scent; it has two new values. Thus Spenser introduces from Ronsard the familiar symbolism which Herrick, Broome and Waller were to echo.

> So passeth in the passing of a day
> Of mortal life the leaf, the bud, the flower;
> Gather therefore the rose while yet 'tis May;

and Marlowe, Campion, Shakespeare, Lodge are lavish of the late Italian-Greek rose, symbol of sensuousness and luxury. When Burns writes

> My luve is like a red, red rose,

it is the rose of the ballads; when Keats writes

> She took me like a child of suckling time
> And cradled me in roses,

they are the roses of Cupid's garland, the red-rose chain of the Renaissance.

The rose is the symbol of loveliness, the outward and visible sign; and here we are touching upon one of the most essential characteristics of poetic diction. " Language, the machine of the poet ", writes Macaulay in his essay on Milton, " is best fitted for its purpose in its rudest state. Nations, like individuals, first perceive and then abstract. They advance from particular images to general terms. Hence the vocabulary of an enlightened society is philosophical, that of a half-civilised people is poetical . . . Generalisation is necessary to the advancement of knowledge: but particularity is indispensable to the creatures of the imagination." As once shops and alehouses had their painted signs that all might know them, so the poets with the aid of similes make abstract ideas intelligible and their images become consecrated by time, conventionalised and transmuted into symbols. Man has a weakness for outward and visible signs, for ceremony and pantomime. The olive is the symbol of peace, the laurel of victory, the crown of kingship, and it is to the natural instinct which bows down before the fasces and the crucifix, that poetry appeals. The modification of the simile into the symbol is worth noting. " Red as a rose " is a pictorial phrase, but in " the rose of youth ", " beauty's rose ", " the expectancy and rose of the fair state ", the descriptive quality is partly lost and a more emotional element has taken its place; similarly phrases such as " dead as a doornail " (Shakespeare) continue to be expressive although we are hardly conscious of the exact meaning. Poetry and proverbs have this in common; they particularise. They employ a vivid image, a concrete instance to express a universal idea. Poetry, in fact, often employs the proverbial method, with this qualification that she treats all things emotionally. If we say that the life of man is like grass, cut down in the evening, we express a truth; substitute the rose for grass and the

appeal becomes at once emotional. " With the great
poet the sense of beauty comes before every other
consideration."   That is to say, the poet names those
objects which have in the past excited the delight, the
desire, the envy, the allegiance of man; those objects
of which to think is to fasten the hand upon the heart.
We may define these words as the idealistic imagery
of poetry.

In oriental poetry precious stones provide the images
of desire, and the usage came to the English poets
through the Bible, particularly the Song of Solomon
and the Revelations.   Dunbar, in some ways curiously
Elizabethan, is lavish of them.   They are found not
only in Marlowe's pagan verse, but also in the sensuous
religious ecstasies and conceits of Phineas Fletcher
and Crashaw and in Traherne's *Centuries of Meditation*.
" Siller and gowd " in the ballads made a similar but
less sensual appeal to their audience, an appeal to the
child rather than to the lover.   *Golden* becomes an
ideal epithet; *silver* is an overworked word as it can
be applied indifferently of colour, of metal and of
sound—the latter puzzles the clowns in *Romeo and
Juliet*—in addition to its original meaning: in *silver
trumpets*, *silver psalteries* two meanings are confused
and made one.

A good example of this imagery of desire (it
extends beyond precious stones) employed for purposes
of description is to be found in the *Venus and Adonis*:

> Full gently now she takes him by the hand,
> A lily prison'd in a gaol of snow,
> Or ivory in an alabaster band,

> So white a friend engirts so white a foe;
> This beauteous combat, wilful and unwilling,
> Show'd like two silver doves that sit a-billing.

But stones, however precious, remain stones; and one prefers a single line of Morris—

> My face made beautiful with my young blood.

Crystal, pearl and ivory are familiar. From 1300, crystal (prized for the goblets and windows of palaces) is the poetic epithet for clear and the conventional description of the eye, and poets ring the changes of fancy on comparisons between pearls and tears.

> Her eyes seen in the tears, tears in the eye
> Both crystals, when they viewed each others' sorrow.

> Whereat her tears began to turn their tide,
> Being prison'd in her eye, like pearls in glass.

But apart from conceits, crystal remains a word consecrated to poetry; in Blake, for example—

> Whether on crystal rocks ye rove
> Beneath the bosom of the sea.

Here lies a hardly realised connection between the crystal rocks and the clearness of the water above and about them; and the epithet affects the whole couplet.
Or again,

> I burst the crystal cabinet
> And like a weeping babe became.

Is it far-fetched to think that the old familiar conceit links *weeping* and *crystal*?

Ivory is coloured by both classical and biblical associations.

> Thy neck is as a tower of ivory.
>> WYCLIF, *Song of Solomon*, 1388.

> Where Beauty, mother to the Muses sits
> And comments volumes with her ivory pen.
>> MARLOWE.

> Thought in her ivory tower gropes in her spinning.
>> DE LA MARE.

Both words have tended to become more idealistic than sensuous.

The same epithet even will read quite differently in

> She's mounted on her milk-white steed.
>> THOMAS THE RHYMER.

and

> With milk-white harts upon an ivory sled.
>> *Tamburlaine.*

The Elizabethan equivalent, *emotionally*, to the " milk-white " of the ballads would be " white as snow ". Milk-white applied to a Hero or Zenocrate suggests something richer—a land flowing with milk and honey. *Silken* is another " luxury epithet ".

Summer also is an example of a word used simply as an image of perfection:

> Such sights as youthful poets dream
> On summer eves by haunted stream.
>> MILTON.

> But thy eternal summer shall not fade.
>> SHAKESPEARE.

> . . . as sweet as ditties highly penned
> Sung by a fair queen in a summer's bower.
>> SHAKESPEARE.

> No spring, nor summer's beauty, hath such grace
> As I have seen in an autumnal face.
>
> DONNE.

> In amorous ditties all a summer's day.
>
> MILTON.

Then as the poetic value of the word is gradually divorced from the actual meaning, the poet can exploit the double significance:

> Can trouble live with April days
> Or sadness in the summer moons.
>
> TENNYSON.

> It never looks like summer here
> On Beeny by the sea!
> But though she saw its look as drear
> Summer it seemed to me.
>
> HARDY.

Gardens, orchards, islands, woods all possess in varying degrees and with slightly different implications an emotional value. Thus a garden carries with it the suggestion of Eden and of the gardens of Adonis and Alcinous. The poet names it idealistically:

> Thy gardens and thy gallant walks
> Continually are green.
>
> *Hierusalem*, 1601.

> I know a little garden close
> Set thick with lily and red rose.
>
> MORRIS.

or by placing, as Spenser does, Time with his scythe in the midst of the garden, or by a reference to the serpent in Paradise, make the beauty more beautiful. Our emotions cling and gather round the word until at last the mere title " A Forsaken Garden " is painful and we need no Swinburne to tell us

> Here there was laughing of old, there was weeping
> Haply, of lovers none ever will know.

The poetic value of " islands " is at first a little difficult to rationalise.   Our emotion about them is not (primarily at any rate) patriotic, despite John of Gaunt and Marvell's

> O thou, that dear and happy Isle
> The *garden* of the world erewhile.

But isles and islands conjure up a powerful visual picture and, over and above this, they suggest remoteness—the Hebrid Isles, the South Seas—and also the warmth and colour of the Mediterranean; the Isles of Greece and

> Beside a pumice isle in Baiae's bay.

To Shelley, more perhaps than to any other poet, they are an ideal image; and they are the key word to some of his most lovely lines.

> It is an isle under Ionian skies.

> Many a green isle needs must be
> In the deep wide sea of misery.

> The halcyons brood around the foamless isles.

Milton has

> Imperious rule of all the seagirt isles.

and

> Or other worlds they seemed, or happy Iles . . .
> Thrice happy Iles——

and

> Of dire Chimeras and enchanted Iles.

And Shakespeare puts a romantic line into the mouth of the love-sick Paris:

> You shall do more than all the *island kings*,
> Unarm great Hector.

And Flecker:

> An isle beside an isle she lay,
> The pale ship anchored in the bay.

When Cleopatra cries " My salad days, when I was green in judgment ", she speaks not the language of poetry but the wit of prose. The poetic version is

> When I would muse in boyhood
> The wild green woods among.

Woods have probably a more patriotic appeal than islands; they suggest English scenery, unlike forests. They have the golden age association of Robin Hood and the outlaws (the greenwood of the ballads), and have been further idealised in *As You Like It* (Act I. Sc. I. 122). And, more important still, it is in the woods that we contemplate the changes of the seasons, the return of spring and the fall of the leaf, and these in their turn are connected, from Homer onwards, with the life of man, with love and with age. Now this is where poetry has the upper hand of prose. Every one has rejoiced over Max Beerbohm's parody of A. C. Benson in *A Christmas Garland*; but the platitudinous reflections upon the seasons which are so common in Dr. Benson's essays were acceptable to an enormous public. They are acceptable to us, intrinsically. All depends upon the presentation. The poet does not explain or employ pictorial detail, but with economy and condensation, employs the word which carries all the implications and suggestions with it, implications too delicate to be defined, " Nous n'irons plus aux bois ". That will tell everything.

For the rest, he concerns himself with the music of his phrases.

Let any one who disbelieves in the traditional poetic values of words, note carefully which words recur and then analyse their emotional and associative significance. Let him compare for example the different effects of mountains and hills: hills have a unique emotional value.

> Fairer than whitest snow on Scythian hills.

> What hills are yon, yon pleasant hills,
> The sun shines sweetly on?—
> O yon are the hills of heaven, he said,
> Where you will never won?

> Home is the sailor, home from sea
> And the hunter home from the hill.

Prospero's line

> Ye elves of hills, brooks, standing lakes and groves,

and Adam's

> Ye hills and dales, ye rivers, woods and plains,

and Wordsworth's

> And O ye Fountains, Meadows, Hills and Groves;

incline one to think that hills, like woods, are coloured by suggestion of England; while to many they revive memories of the very emotional hymn

> There is a green hill far away,

and (more justifiably) of the psalm

> I will lift up my eyes unto the hills from whence cometh my help,

and (more significantly) of the old rhyme

> Over the hills and far away.

In Housman they occur continually (a strong proof of
the " English " association):

> What are those blue remembered hills?

> And standing hills, long to remain,
> Shared their short-lived comrade's pain.

The value of the " L " sound also must not be ignored.

The moon, the nightingale and the rose, orchards
and gardens, amber and ivory, kings and queens, the
months and stars and seasons, these are the current
coin of poetry. Even in *The Thirteenth Caesar*
orchards, golden apples and green leaves are the
favourite and ideal images. They are in themselves
beautiful, poetic subjects, and possess secondary
emotional implications. Compare this metaphor of
Bishop King—

> At night, when I betake to rest
> Next morn I rise nearer my West
> Of life, almost by eight hours' sail,

with the more symbolical usage of Wordsworth—

> And stepping Westward seemed to be
> A kind of heavenly destiny,

and in Housman—

> Comrade, look not on the West,
> 'Twill have the heart out of your breast;

> The winds out of the west land blow,
> My friends have breathed them there,

and in Mary Coleridge's mystical poem—

> Low let me lie, where the dead dog lies,
>   Ere I sit me down again at a feast,
> When there passes a woman with the West in her eyes
>   And a man with his back to the East,

F

and De la Mare's epitaph—

> But beauty vanishes, beauty passes
> However rare—rare it be,
> And when I crumble who will remember
> The lady of the West Country?

The West is at once a land of heart's desire (Westward Ho!), and the place where the sun sets (with the idea of death, as in the soldiers' phrase "gone West"). Poets temper our delight in natural objects with pity, and suggest a symbolical relation with the life of men.

One epithet is as a rule more telling in poetry than two. Images and symbols, equally, stand better alone. In Swinburne they jostle one another and clash like ill-assorted colours; in his verses (where each stanza is as a wave breaking upon shingle, neither more nor less musical than the last, an infinite series with no appointed beginning or end) the grapes of pleasure, ashes of desire, poppies of forgetfulness, roses of love have no decorative value. All are steeped in the same emotional honey. Particular associations are dulled by frequent epithets. No word speaks for itself but joins in the general chorus. There are few *solo* lines in Swinburne. That feeling of inevitability which is so essential to great poetry is falsely created by the movement and the brilliant interweaving of insistent rhymes. There are no contrasts, no subtle juxtapositions to heighten the values of the words, except that now and again the poet exchanges the attributes and symbols of his abstracts, giving Time a gift of tears, Grief a glass that ran, or naming the white rose of the spirit

and the red lily of love, the rose-leaves of December,
the frosts of June, the lees of pleasure, the grapes of
pain. But the individuality of the words has been
sacrificed and these facile paradoxes pass almost
unheeded. Let any passionate disciple of his art call,
as he reads, the adjectives to account, or note the
use of the word " blood ", which reaches the height
of insensitiveness in such a passage as

> From boy's pierced throat and girl's pierced bosom
> Drips, reddening round the blood-red blossom,
> The slow delicious bright soft blood.[1]

Swinburne was seduced by the Elizabethans: even
Shakespeare provides a precedent for his stanza:

> Alas, a crimson river of warm blood,
> Like to a bubbling fountain stirred with wind,
> Doth rise and fall between thy rosy lips,
> Coming and going with thy honey breath.
> > (*Titus Andronicus*, cp. *Lucrece*, 1737.)

In Swinburne's pages Dionysus and Jesus Christ
join hands, and pagan and Roman Catholic images and
symbols are mingled together. And as this diction
is employed for the treatment of erotic subjects and
sensuous suggestions, one cannot wonder at the
fabulous enchantment which his poetry had for the
undergraduates of that date and the schoolboys of
yesterday. It is the reaction against this diction
which has made the hard words of Donne so satisfying.
Thus history repeats itself.

---

[1] " *Blood* is made as light of in some of these old dramas as *money* in a
modern sentimental comedy " (Charles Lamb).

Swinburne and his poetic parasites debased the Elizabethan currency which Keats revived, exactly as the eighteenth century debased the Latin coinage of Milton. And the heirs of Swinburne are—the inventors of serial-titles, sentimental songs, cheap fiction, the authors of film captions. These employ the emotional symbols and imagery into which the essence of poetry has for many centuries been distilled —*Lily of the Dust*, *The Last Rose of Summer*, *The Garden of Allah*, *Coral Island*.

The affinity between titles of books and poetry is worth noticing. It is significant that titles are in many cases quotations—*Time is whispering*, *The Crystal Cabinet*, *Antic Hay*, *Pipers and a Dancer*, *The Painted Veil*. Titles suggest much in little; they are at once a label and an enigma. The letters of the phrase harmonise and bind the words together as in a musical chord. In all these respects a title is potentially poetry. Consider, for example, the adjective *green* in book titles; always it has the poetic or secondary value, the associations which it does not possess in prose. Thus *Green Mansions*, *The Green Mirror*, *The House with Green Shutters*, have a curiously romantic effect.

The language of poetry has at the present time been universally exploited for popular purposes, and a conviction prevails that poetry, if any function or future yet remains for it, will be occupied with raiding and sequestrating portions of the new, immense, ill-governed empire of prose. Mr. Eliot is a master of guerilla warfare. Eventually perhaps social conditions will have established other objects exciting envy and delight, factories instead of gardens, wire-drawers instead of princes, fly-wheels instead of roses, from which the poet may draw his images. That time has not yet come and, in their context, the old symbols and subjects are, for a little space, still proof against vulgar associations. Cherry blossom may suggest Devonshire to one man, Tchekov to another and boot polish to a third (if ejaculated alone and unashamed by the psycho-analyst), but will, in a lyric, retain its original purity.

Two Victorian sonnet sequences provide a stimulating contrast in poetic method; sister sequences as different in character as Martha and Mary. Rossetti's *House of Life* abounds in idealistic imagery and rejoices in the conventions and traditional symbols of poetry, in allegory, in personification, in emotional epithets, in painful repetitions, in yearning polysyllables.

> Behold, this crocus is a withering flame;
> This snowdrop, snow; this apple blossom's part
> To breed the fruit that breeds the serpent's art.
> Nay, for these spring flowers, turn thy face from them,
> Nor gaze till on the year's last lily stem
> The white cup shrivels round the golden heart.
>
> Yet for this hour I still may here be stayed
> And see the gold air and the silver fade
> And the last bird fly into the last light.
>
> O love, my love; if I no more should see
> Thyself, nor on the earth the shadow of thee,
> Nor image of thine eyes in any spring—
> How then should sound upon life's darkening slope
> The ground-whirl of the perished leaves of hope,
> The wind of death's imperishable wing?

In his diction Rossetti shows both the art and the licence of the poet. His success as a sonneteer lies in his way of making the sestet a second wave which rides on the back of the octave, becoming one with it as they break in a line of foam and land one firmly and triumphantly upon the verge of the shingle. But Meredith in the seizains of *Modern Love* has a different tale to tell and a different way of telling it. He makes the first incursion upon the domain of prose, and by a wonderful *tour de force* squeezes poetry out of a stony stage situation. As in the sonnets and tragedies of Shakespeare, passion and jealousy and unfaithfulness are the subject. Like Donne he strives to combine reason and emotion. He anticipates such a piece as T. S. Eliot's *Portrait of a Lady*. *Modern Love*, once made one's own, satisfies more moods than *The House of Life*. The philosophy and the psychology are confirmed by every new experience, and Meredith's compact and emphatic phrasing seems, at each reading, to shift a burden from the heart. The style is rich in metaphors and at moments symbolical, but it is less luxuriant, less lyrical than his prose.

I have digressed to mark this contrast because in this chapter the reminder may prove salutary that there are two sides to the medal and that poetry can be, and in the greatest writers always is, something more than " poetical ".

The days of the potato are, rumour has it, numbered. The original specimen introduced by Sir Walter Raleigh has been crossed and inbred so unceasingly that unless a new tuber is brought from Guiana, the

vegetable will die out. A similar calamity has over-
taken the lily and rose of poetry. For more than
five centuries they have blossomed and blown and gone
to seed and unfolded their buds again.

> Sweet rois of vertew and of gentilness,
> Delytsum lily of everie lustines.
>
> DUNBAR.

> The lily and the rose most sweetly strange
> Upon her dimpled cheeks do strive for change.
>
> FORD.

> Queen rose of the rosebud garden of girls,
> Queen lily and rose in one.
>
> TENNYSON.

> Decking her coverlet with sprigs of gold,
> Roses, and lilies white that best befit her.
>
> BRIDGES.

What shall the poet do? The cyclamen and calceolaria
cannot compete with the lily and the rose in the
Muses' garden. They are not symbols; their value
is not emotional but visual. The other flowers of
poetry are gathered for us — by Spenser, by Milton,
by Edith Sitwell—*for their names' sake*. They are
musical, they are decorative; but we make acquaintance with them in later life, not in our childhood.
" Mr. Locke has somewhere observed (I quote from
Burke's *Reflections*) that most general words, those
belonging to virtue and vice, good and evil especially,
are taught before the particular modes of action to
which they belong, are presented to the mind, and with
them the love of the one and the abhorrence of the
other; for the minds of children are so ductile that a
nurse or any person about a child by seeming pleased

or displeased with anything or *even any word*, may give the disposition of the child a similar turn." Our emotions are engaged on behalf of the commonplaces of poetry in the same way from earliest times, and we remain faithful to them. We believe that it is passing fair to be a king and are moved by the ravishing division of the nightingale before we have heard his song.

All this may seem much ado about nothing, but I have insisted upon the recurrence of these consecrated images, because the usage is an essential characteristic of poetry and distinguishes it from prose. When we find words so used in prose, as in the following passage of Donne, we may call it poetic writing.

. . . . all the four Monarchies, with all their thousands of years, and all the powerful Kings, and all the beautiful Queens of this world, were but as a bed of flowers, some gathered at six, some at seven, some at eight—all in one morning in respect of this day.

When a generation labels everything as " superb " or " divine ", when a man says " damn " or " hell ", the actual meaning of the word is secondary to its emotional value; the word becomes a symbol of pleasure or disgust. The use of language in poetry is extraordinarily similar.

These images I have called outward and visible signs, for there exist also (with no reference to Plato) poetic ideas; abstract qualities which appeal to the senses; brightness, softness, sweetness, stillness, and, more subtly, remoteness or distance. If we may not call these qualities of beauty, they are simply causes of pleasure and approval, and the majority of adjectives in poetry are chosen with reference to them, where, like the images, they acquire certain associations and significance. This is the subject of a later chapter.

The famous lines of Nash—

> Brightness falls from the air;
> Queens have died young and fair;
> Dust hath closed Helen's eye,

give in little the three devices of poetry. First, we have the abstract poetic idea, then the general romantic word with emotional associations, the outward and visible sign, and then thirdly " the local habitation and name ". Helen is chosen as the prototype of queens as the rose is of flowers.

The poetic idea of remoteness is, as we have seen, the explanation of the appeal which islands make, the appeal which lies in Marvell's lines—

> Where the remote Bermudas ride
> In the ocean's bosom unespied.

The name is half real, half ideal.

In the following quotations we find a name consecrated by the poets until it becomes a traditional symbol:

> Where e'er thy bones are hurl'd,
> Whether beyond the stormy Hebrides,
> Where thou perhaps under the humming [1] tide
> Visit'st the bottom of the monstrous world.

James Thomson, imitator of Milton, has in the romantic *Castle of Indolence*:

> As when some shepherd of the Hebrid isles
> Placed far amid the melancholy main.

---

[1] Humming. So in Milton's MS. Afterwards altered to *whelming*; the original epithet, stolen from *Pericles*, is more poetic.

and Collins—

> Round the moist marge of each cold Hebrid isle.

Wordsworth writes—

> Breaking the silence of the seas
> Among the farthest Hebrides,

which Poe plagiarises—

> Ah, by no sound are stirred those trees,
> They palpitate like the chill seas
> Among the misty Hebrides;

and the line in the Canadian boating song—

> And we in dreams behold the Hebrides,

however exact in its original meaning, rings emotionally, symbolically, in our ears.

The fact that Boswell and Johnson and many other more susceptible spirits since their time have toured the Hebrides, does not affect the poetic value of the name.   Whether we have seen them ourselves or not, they are, in their poetic setting " fairy lands forlorn ", as remote and desirable as a " country far beyond the stars ".   The names of poetry are ideal names.   The appeal is to our imagination.   What does Homer tell us of Helen?   That Aphrodite herself set a chair for her; that the old men at the gate thought such a creature worthy the long pains of war.   She is a vision, as in *Faustus*, a symbol, a prototype.   When I read Broome's lines—

> Now Helen lives alone in fame
> And Cleopatra's but a name,

I am not moved as I am by those of Nash or by Villon's ballade, because Shakespeare has made Cleopatra

too individual a character, subtle and complex. The
name is no more a symbol than Anna Karenina.
Aristotle lays it down that the personages of tragedy
should be of high degree; he is speaking of poetic
drama and he is right. Hedda Gabler is no less tragic
than Oedipus, but she is the creation not of poetry but
of psychology; in poetic drama our emotions are
already fastened in advance upon the characters or
types; kings and queens, the heroic and the beautiful,
figures moving in a world remote from our own.
Hamlet is a hybrid form, combining verse soliloquies
with realistic and illuminating dialogue in prose, and
has the best of both worlds. Cordelia and Miranda
are ideal, poetic creatures, and it is fruitless to conjecture, as Bradley does, how Imogen would have made
answer to Lear.

I have already cited *Mrs. Dalloway*, a recent novel
by Virginia Woolf, as an example of prose employing
poetic method; and in it is to be found a description
of *Bond Street* of the ideal kind which we are treating;
not a description of the Bond Street that the Londoner
knows, but a fantasia, a poetic interpretation of all that
Bond Street symbolises: it becomes an ideal name as
the Hebrides, as Ormus, as Arabia or Arcady are ideal
names.

History and mythology are the royal purses from
which this poetic coin is drawn. The name may be an
individual one—in conversation we speak of an Adonis,
an Alexander, a Napoleon—as it is in Virgil's

> Si qua fata aspera rumpas!
> Tu Marcellus eris,

where Marcellus is an exemplar of all whom the gods have loved, as Helen is of beauty. But more often the *historical* name is not that of a particular person but that of a family or dynasty: there the associations gather and multiply with time: the appeal is to the past.

The poetry of these names is most subtly and fully expressed in *A la Recherche du Temps Perdu*. In the two volumes of *Le Côté de Guermantes*, Marcel Proust describes the intense feeling of a young man for the names and titles of the old aristocracy, names whose very syllables seemed to contain forest glades and gothic belfries. The mere sound of the words La Princesse de Parmes filled the air with the scent of violets; and like many other young men he falls in love with the Duchesse de Guermantes for her name's sake, as the incarnation of the splendid and historic past, a fairy not a woman.

A l'âge où les Noms, nous offrant l'image de l'inconnaissable que nous avons versé en eux, dans le même moment où ils désignent aussi pour nous un lieu réel, nous forcent par là à identifier l'un à l'autre au point que nous partons chercher dans une cité une âme qu'elle ne peut contenir mais que nous n'avons plus le pouvoir d'expulser de son nom, ce n'est pas seulement aux villes et aux fleuves qu'ils donnent une individualité, comme le font les peintures allégoriques, ce n'est pas seulement l'univers physique qu'ils diaprent de différences qu'ils peuplent de merveilleux, c'est aussi l'univers social: alors chaque château, chaque hôtel ou palais fameux a sa dame, ou sa fée, comme les forêts leurs génies et leurs divinités les eaux.

The best parallel to be found in English is a

magnificent and little known passage in a speech of Chief Justice Crewe:

Time hath his revolutions. There must be a period and an end of all temporal things, *finis rerum*, an end of names and dignities and whatsoever is terrene, and why not of De Vere? For where is Bohun; where is Mowbray; where is Mortimer; nay, which is more and most of all, where is Plantagenet? They are entombed in the urns and sepulchres of mortality.

Despite the familiar prose rhythms this is poetry. This emotional use of names and their associations, method of particularising, of seeking for signs and symbols, is, in the truest sense, poetic diction. This peroration of Crewe is like a stained-glass window full of the shields and armorial bearings of ladies dead and lovely knights. Each colour and quartering has an allegorical or historic significance.

Names are the definitions which we give to the indefinable. We fasten upon them our superfluous and unemployed emotions and desires. They excite the curiosity and imagination of the child. Every name is at once mysterious and full of suggestion, which is the most stimulating combination. They are the resort of poets as they are the refuge of the idealist, and of all the poets Milton has employed them with most art and cunning. His " muster rolls of charmed names " have two values, one of sound, one of association. Macaulay remarked the second and was deaf to the first.

Yet the line

And Eleale to the Asphaltic pool,

and the oft quoted digression (an oasis) in *Paradise
Regained*—

> And Ladies of th' *Hesperides*, that seem'd
> Fairer then feign'd of old, or fabl'd since
> Of Fairy Damsels met in Forest wide
> By knights of *Logres*, or of *Lyones*,
> *Lancelot* or *Pelleas*, or *Pellenore*,

are most delicate and elaborate harmonies of letters.
These five lines distil all the beauty of *The Faery Queen*.
The other words no less than the names, are designed
to recall the past: and the names themselves move us
like those of Bohun, Mowbray and De Vere above, as
Guermantes, Saintrailles and Guise moved Proust.
We cannot define that emotion or put it into words.
Milton's names here are like Rossetti's " five sweet
symphonies ", but he more often exploits not the literal
but the syllabic value of names.　English is none too
rich in high-sounding polysyllables, and Milton by
naming Atabalipa, Gallaphrone, Adiabene, Salman-
assar, Artaxata, Taprobane, Melesigenes, remedies
the defect, varies the movement and weight of his
verse, and emulates the Aeschylean iambic.　Webster
achieves similar effects in his partiality for such words
as eternally, perpetually, irrecoverably, irregular, fantastical, geometrical, but they tend less to add weight
than to loosen the texture of his verse.

Max Beerbohm complains somewhere that Pater
writes English as if it was a dead language, and this
would be a true criticism of Miltonic verse.　Apart
from the Graecisms, Latinisms and periphrases, the
artificial order of words, Milton carefully avoids the

natural and familiar even in his names: Homer, for instance, he calls Maeonides; King Arthur, Uther's son; Pharaoh, Busiris; Vulcan, Mulciber: Macedonian becomes Emathian, Italian Ausonian. He names an unknown province or town, where another poet would name the continent. To enjoy him one needs an atlas at one elbow and a history at the other. But his immense learning is the foundation on which the fabric of his poetry is raised; he is not, like his imitator Gray, " tall by walking on tiptoe ", and it was inevitable that a blind man should see the world through the spectacles of books. Behind each of his capital names there lies some particular story or reference, like the unseen bodyguard of a king. The average reader is un-conscious of this and contents himself with enjoying the noises and having vague emotions about the past or (as also when he hears the superb catalogue of nations who witnessed the gift of tongues upon the apostles at Pentecost), responds to the romance of the East, or, repeating the names of the planets and starry constellations, seems for a moment to dally with infinity.

For in the utterance of a name is power, creative, possessive power: " *Demogorgon* " raises a spirit; " John " turns a human being into a puppet, a footman. As Miss Harrison describes it in her *Reminiscences*, " I had a child's magical habit of mind; and if I could get the name *exactly* (viz. Lady Jane) I should somehow possess the person. To name is to create. ' And God said to the light, " Light " (He named it), and there *was* light '."

Marlowe had been the first to appreciate the syllabic effects of capital names; one can witness the realisation coming upon him almost unawares with the line, " To ride in triumph through Persepolis ", over which he lingers amorously, and afterwards repeats the cadence with the refrain, " To entertain divine Zenocrate ".   But one cannot say of his names as Macaulay does of Milton's that " every one of them is the first link in a long train of associated ideas ". Inspired perhaps by the pageant of capital names which headed the proclamations of the Tudor monarchs, he exploited popular patriotism and allegiance in such a passage as

> We here do crown thee monarch of the East,
> Emperor of Asia and of Persia,
> Great lord of Media and Armenia:
> Duke of Africa and Albania,
> Mesopotamia and of Parthia,
> East India and the late-discovered isles.

These names belong to the same class of words as Marlowe's sensuous imagery, the silver and gold, pearl and ivory, sun and moon and stars, scarlet and milk-white, with which he inlays his pages.   Milton, the Puritan, exchanged the appeal of learning for that of luxury, of books for that of courts and palaces.   Yet Marlowe lays his finger on the ultimate value of a name in poetry, in his " What is beauty saith my sufferings then? "   It is the one thought, one wonder, one grace,

> Which into words no virtue can digest,

that can be distilled into a name, whether it be Zenocrate or Guermantes or Rose Aylmer.

Ah, what avails the sceptred race!
Ah, what the form divine!
What every virtue, every grace!
Rose Aylmer, all were thine.

The name is a musical one, otherwise it would not
gain as it does from the repetition in the second verse.
Rose adds the suggestion of beauty and the colour of
youth to the sceptred race and form divine.   We may
glance here at Aristotle's dictum that the tragic hero
belongs to those of great repute and prosperity (τῶν
ἐν μεγάλῃ δόξῃ ὄντων καὶ εὐτυχίᾳ) and also: ἐπεὶ δὲ
μίμησίς ἐστιν ἡ τραγῳδία βελτιόνων, ἡμᾶς δεῖ μιμεῖσθαι
τοὺς ἀγαθοὺς εἰκονογράφους. καὶ γὰρ ἐκεῖνοι ἀποδιδόντες τὴν
ἰδίαν μορφὴν ὁμοίους ποιοῦντες καλλίους γράφουσι.   The
poetic device in this case is to transfer our emotions
to an imaginary name, of which the poet suggests just
enough for us to class it with the names of history
and mythology.

Every man can for himself compare, say, La Belle
Dame Sans Merci with Faustine, or Rose Aylmer with
De la Mare's Lady of the West Country, and decide
what is the exact advantage or reverse of the name,
analyse the very delicate gradations of intensity between
the general and the particular.   One does not wish
that the ancient mariner or the leech-gatherer or the
solitary reaper had been christened by their creators.
Why ?   Because they are, in a sense, objective poems
Their appeal lies in a certain remoteness.   The solitary reaper is a voice, the leech-gatherer a lonely spirit,
and their poet a contemplator.   But with Wordsworth
we come upon new developments and uses of names.

G

In his essay on epitaphs there is a remarkable revelation. " In an obscure corner of a country churchyard (he writes) I once espied, half overgrown with hemlock and nettles, a very small stone laid upon the ground being nothing more than the name of the deceased with the date of birth and death, importing that it was an infant which had been born one day and died the following. I know not how far the reader may be in sympathy with me, but more awful thoughts of rights conferred, of hopes awakened, of remembrances stealing and vanishing, were imported to my mind by that inscription there before my eyes, than by any other that it has been my lot to meet with upon a tombstone." Epitaphs are a spur to the imagination but to few of us can an epitaph have brought such emotion as this. His point of view makes a striking contrast to names with which we have been dealing. Wordsworth it is true, adopted the religious mysticism of Vaughan; he is shaken by religious excitement, not like one who finds romantic pleasure in tracing the inscription on the tomb of a Turberville. None the less the passage above is a good commentary on the Lucy poems.

> She lived alone and few could tell
> When Lucy ceased to be;
> But she is in her grave, and oh
> The difference to me.

What is the value of the name here and what in

> Sally is gone who was so kindly,
> Sally is gone from Hannacker Mill;

or

> The night is freezing fast,
> To-morrow comes December;
> And winterfalls of old
> Are with me from the past;
> And chiefly I remember
> How Dick would hate the cold.

There is no mystery, but instead intimacy. In Belloc's lines, it is true, there is a secret appeal to the past: for Sally is a last century name and mills are indispensable to Victorian engravings. The theme is the familiar one—" Beauty passes ". But Sally and Hannacker Mill are, in effect, more realistic than symbolical. The local name, be it Ludlow or Kentucky or Grantchester or Innisfree, carries conviction: we respond to a personal appeal and transfer the sentiment which every one nourishes for certain places. Some people resent this subjective local poetry.

The Tom, Dick and Harry of *A Shropshire Lad* —Dick who hates the cold is the child of Dick the shepherd blowing his nail in *Love's Labour's Lost*— correspond (despite their criminal tendencies) to Thestylis and Corydon of the artificial world.

> The youth towards his fancy
> Would turn his brow of tan,
> And Tom would pair with Nancy
> And Dick step off with Fan.

The ideal is passed upon us as real.

As regards capital names the saying of Longinus is true, which has already been noted with reference to

ordinary words, that a homely expression is sometimes
much more telling than elegant language.   Clunbury,
Yarrow and Kirconnel Lea may be more telling than
Arcady, Oxus or Bellerus old: the John Anderson,
Mary Morison, fair Lesley of Burns than the Corinna,
Electra, Perenna of Herrick.   For poets invite us to
see the world, now through one, now through the other
end of the telescope: painfully close at hand or infinitely remote and beautiful.   In the first case they
have the prose writer to compete with, in the second
they rule alone.   A good test of one's own preferences
in the use of names may be taken, by noting the
reaction to Bridges' poem—

> I never shall love the snow again
> Since Maurice died.

To many the intimacy of the appeal is inartistic:
the name Maurice is more personal in this context than
the Dick of *Last Poems* who is partly ideal, partly
symbolical.

The elegies of three classical scholars, Milton,
Gray and Arnold, show the gradations between the
natural and artificial in this respect.   *Lycidas* advances
upon Spenser's *Astrophel* in that it is a lament for a
drowned friend and not a tribute to a deceased patron.
Although the grief is more melodious than piercing,
feeling at least breaks through in the incongruous
attack upon the corrupted clergy.   But the names are
Damoetas, Orpheus, Amaryllis, Panope and Alpheus.
If Milton's elegy is more a poem than an expression of
grief, Gray's elegy is more a sermon than a poem.

The style is Latin rather than Greek, but it is composed in a country churchyard, and the atmosphere is English. Above all it is significant that in the stanza

> Some village Hampden that with dauntless breast
> The little tyrant of his fields withstood,
> Some mute inglorious Milton here may rest,
> Some Cromwell guiltless of his country's blood,

the names first chosen by Gray were Cato, Tully and Caesar. They were rejected in favour of native ones.

The naturalising process was completed by Matthew Arnold. He did not disguise Oxfordshire in a Sicilian mantle: there is none of the confusion of *Lycidas*. He " spoke out " and named Thames and Cumner and Hinksey and Bablock - hithe. The clumsiness of calling his hero Thyrsis and a shepherd was eased by the seventeenth - century story of the Scholar Gipsy already told. One can contrast also the flowers Arnold names (and his method of naming them) —musk carnations, sweet-william, loose-strife, snapdragon and bluebells—with Milton's more elaborate and Elizabethan catalogue. *Thyrsis*, although a pastoral elegy, lies nearer *Love in a Valley* than Theocritus.

To return to Wordsworth, his figures are named because they have a story to tell, and in his determination to winnow away all except the elemental fact, to arrive at absolute simplicity and purity, the poet isolates and sets apart single creatures, characters they cannot be called, and naming them makes them his own, identifying the name with the story. They are individual figures, not symbolical, not ideal; figures in a parable. Wordsworth heads *Peter Bell* with the quotation—

> What's in a name?
> Brutus will start a spirit as soon as Caesar,

which, as far as poetry is concerned, is as false as Shakespeare's other dictum on the name of the rose. Although Wordsworth succeeded in throwing a certain colouring of the imagination over incidents and situations from common life, even including Peter Bell, yet his names can only possess the import and potency which he himself creates for them, not that which is rubbed and brightened by many ages, which rings with the echoes of many tongues. But this recompense is his, a certain poignancy, and a personal note of appeal. With their aid Lucy can hold her own against the heavenly Una with her milk-white lamb and the lovely lady Christabel.

" By raising nature to the level of human thought ", writes Pater of Wordsworth, " he gives it power and expression : he subdues man to the level of nature, and gives him thereby a certain breadth and coolness and solemnity." His figures are, in fact, creatures of their environment, personifications of the spirits of the lakes and hills, like the pagan divinities of Greece. For Wordsworth yearning for a sight of Proteus rising from the sea, was far more fundamentally possessed by natural religion than Keats, who, Clare complained, " saw behind every bush a thrumming Apollo ". A modern writer, Mr. T. F. Powys, is curiously Wordsworthian in this respect; his creatures are part of the surroundings in which they live. But whereas Wordsworth walks by silent tarns and bare mountains, Mr. Powys's way lies among rich meadows and rank pastures, and he has glimpses not of Proteus or old Triton but of Pan and Silenus and satyrs with cloven heel. He is concerned not with the essential passions of the heart but with the lusts of the flesh. A Freudian interpretation of rustic life is more acceptable to the modern palate than Wordsworthian mysticism, but I do not believe that the mythology and animistic religion of Greece has at any time fulfilled a need and become part and parcel of English poetry. It remains an ornament. The folk-lore and legends of Ireland, although inferior in quality, to some extent, provide a parallel: they have inspired nothing in literature comparable to the epigrams in the Greek anthology but more vitality lingers in their superstitions.

The names of the gods and heroes of Greece and Rome are the last upon which I shall touch. From this treasury every poet has begged, borrowed and stolen. The Renaissance translators filled the pockets of the University wits—and they were spendthrifts indeed. Let us take some general examples:

> violets dim
> But sweeter than the lids of Juno's eyes
> Or Cytherea's breath.

> Tasting of Flora and the country green.

> Kiss me: so! Thus hung Jove on Leda's neck
> And sucked divine ambrosia from her lips.

> When Dorian shepherds sang to Proserpine.

> It may be we shall touch the Happy Isles
> And see the great Achilles whom we know.

These are the names of the ideal kind of which I have already spoken, names appealing to our imagination and our emotions about the past. Thus Landor's sentence, " Helen died, Laodomeia died, Rhodope the beloved of Jupiter went before ", is poetic writing and the exact counterpart of the quotation from Justice Crewe.

To the Elizabethans, who feasted upon the *Metamorphoses* of Ovid, classical mythology provided opportunities for conceits and instances and pictorial ornament. The fare was exactly suited to an adolescent state of society which saw men as gods. Painters and embroiderers hung the walls with the amours of Jupiter, Phoebus and Pan, and the poets wrote with one eye on the arras. Thus Cleopatra is described as " o'erpicturing that Venus where we see the fancy outwork nature ", and is herself the subject of the hangings in Imogen's bed-chamber. Chaucer has classical imitations and artificial descriptions (of daybreak, for instance), but he does not attempt the detailed embroidery of the later poets. The ornamental way of writing is pleasing enough for its own sake from Spenser's *Prothalamium* down to Housman's; but the ornament remains external, an imitation, a grace licensed to poets, as rouge and powder are to women. Hamlet found painting, and Johnson *Lycidas*, distasteful.

The value of the mythological name is best examined by comparing Swinburne's

> When all the stars make gold of all the air

with Tennyson's

> Now lies the earth all Danaë to the stars.

In the first the lingering and painful effect of the monosyllables and the repetition of " all "—the emphases
fall on the strong words—are suitable to the tone of
the poem. Tennyson, apart from the apt and ideal
interpretation of the old myth, which is suitable also
to the context, love being the subject, carries one
back with the name into the dim past, and by naming
the earth and the stars sets the whole on a grand scale,
suggests the universal.   But the line remains a conceit,
beautiful for its own sake, and not perhaps out of
harmony with the porphyry font and the elaborate,
somewhat theatrical, setting of the poem.

> The fair humanities of old religion,
> The power, the beauty, and the majesty,
> That had their haunts in dale or piny mountain,
> Or forest, by slow stream, or pebbly spring,
> Or chasms, or watery depths; all these have vanished ;
> They live no longer in the faith of reason,
> But still the heart doth need a language, still
> Doth the old instinct bring back the old names.

That is the conclusion of the whole matter.   Poetic
diction is no more than a consecrated code of symbols
and passwords, the language of the heart.   Whether it
be the rose or Rhodope—

> still
> Doth the old instinct bring back the old names.

IV

ADJECTIVES

> *Caperwit.* I will maintain it against
> A bundle of grammarians, in poetry
> The substantive itself cannot subsist
> Without its adjective.
> *Friend.* But for all that
> These words would sound more full methinks that are not
> So larded.
>
> JAMES SHIRLEY, *The Changes*, 1632.

ADJECTIVES ARE SIRENS; they betray all whom
their music beguiles. Enslave them and you
are master of the poetic art. Their talents are four:
they have sound, meaning, decorative value and
emotional value. The poet will harmonise as many
of the four as he can. When selecting an adjective
for the second or fourth reason, he will be not a little
influenced by the sound value. That is to say, where
the epithet is used primarily for its meaning (to
amplify a noun), a synonym frequently offers itself
and sound will be the deciding factor, while in the
case of emotional value, the effect may be enhanced
by selecting a monosyllable rather than a polysyllable
or a long rather than a short vowel sound. The
decorative epithet may be paradoxical as in the Sitwells,
or a descriptive double form, " dewy-tasselled " for
instance, or archaic (" lorn ", " antique "), when it
tends to acquire an emotional value. The despotic
powers of the adjective will be realised if we compare
" faint stars " with " burning stars ", or " O Eastern
star " (Shakespeare) with " the hispid stars " (Mr.

Harold Acton).   Although one adjective will often do twice as much work as two, some poets will be found who prefer quantity to quality.   Where the poet is not lavish of figures in his style, the verbs and substantives give the gist of the verse, and the adjectives the emotional tone, a process which is rare in prose.   We have seen how certain words are rich in association, and how the poets juggle with traditional symbols and create new ones for themselves.   A similar associative process often lies concealed behind an epithet and is the secret of its value.   We will consider first the emotional significance of adjectives and the peculiarities of the poetic usage.

As an example of this characteristic of poetic diction let us attempt to analyse the striking line:

> A bracelet of bright hair about the bone.

The dramatic excitement of the whole poem, the vividness of the visual picture, need no remark; the alliteration is subtle—the four hard B's contrasting with the numerous, varied vowel sounds, just as the bone contrasts with the bright hair.   " Bright hair "; the phrase is alive; it recurs in poetry.   One recalls Cressida's " Tear my bright hair ", " The bright-haired sun " which Collins borrowed from Milton, and " The bright hair . . . of some fierce Maenad " in Shelley.   More notably still:

> A shadow like an angel with bright hair
> Dabbled in blood.

Here there is another of the underground connections in which the words suggest and depend on one

another, giving the impression of inevitability. The
link between " angel " and " bright " is strong.

> Speak again, bright angel.

> Angels are bright still, though the brightest fell.

> An angel beautiful and bright.

> Bright-harnessed angels.

> Bright
> With something of an angel light.

Yet this angelic brightness differs in some way from
the brightness in Donne's line. The one is the
brightness of mortality, the other of immortality.
Let us take the first again. Light and darkness, this
is one of the most elemental facts in human existence,
perhaps the first which our consciousness grasps.
" Let there be light and there was light " is sublime,
as the cry of *Samson Agonistes* is terrible:

> O dark, dark, dark amid the blaze of noon,
> Irrecoverably dark,

and for the same reason; because the division into
light and darkness is a universal mystery and law.
All words which suggest the one or the other will have
power to shake us, to rejoice or terrify. But further,
light and darkness have always formed an analogy
with life and death. Apart from the love poem of
Catullus—" Nox est perpetua una dormienda ", one
has but to instance our own phrase " The shadow of
death ".

In the Elizabethan age, death was sudden and life was not merely existence. " Timor mortis conturbat me " had been the motto and knell of the Middle Ages. The Elizabethans lived in the sun, and their shadow lay beside them. We shall find the word " Bright " ever and again on the lips of the dramatists. Hear Charmian—

> Finish, good lady, the bright day is done,
> And we are for the dark ;

which turns Tennyson's farewell to a faint echo. Hear Hippolito—

> It cannot be
> Such a bright taper should burn out so soon,

or the dying Orgilus—

> A mist hangs o'er mine eyes, the sun's bright splendour
> Is clouded in an everlasting shadow.

Hear Giovanni as he stabs his sister—

> Be dark, bright sun, and make this midday night,

or Wolsey—

> I shall fall
> Like a bright exhalation in the evening
> And no man see me more ;

and in Marston—

> Death's at thy window, awake, bright Mellida,

or Vindici—

> My study's ornament, thou shell of death,
> Once the bright face of my betrothed lady,

or in Nash—

> Brightness falls from the air:
> Queens have died young and fair ;

and Ben Jonson—

> Have you seen but a bright lily grow
> Before rude hands have touched it?

and Shakespeare—

> So quick bright things come to confusion,

and then in the light of these—

> A bracelet of bright hair about the bone.

The contrast and the symbolism are the same. "Bright" is the poetic word for "alive", symbolical, as the rose, of beauty and vitality. In this sense we light upon it everywhere; in Vaughan and Milton, in Wordsworth, Coleridge and Arnold. In "Strange fits of passion I have known" the symbolical usage occurs.

> My horse moved on: hoof after hoof
> He raised and never stopped,
> When down behind the cottage roof
> At once the bright moon dropped.

> What fond and wayward thoughts will slide
> Into a lover's head.
> "O mercy", to myself I cried,
> "If Lucy should be dead."

The style is un-Elizabethan, bald instead of bare, but the symbolism is the same. *Julius Caesar* has a vivid line:

> It is the bright day that brings forth the adder.

The adder suggests something dark and deadly and is in strong contrast with the associations of *bright*. I do not forget that the Elizabethans have other ways of putting the night and day, life and death analogy. I do not forget Macbeth's " Out, out, brief candle ", or Othello's " Put out the light ", or Cleopatra's " Our lamp is spent ", or the cry of Leontes, " Stars, stars, and all eyes else dead coals ". Here also lies the secret of

> Cover her face. Mine eyes dazzle. She died young.

It is simple and direct, naked as ordinary speech, but heightened by the one word " dazzle ", which suggests the intolerable brightness and beauty of the face.

The relation between light and life, bright and beautiful, crops up in many different contexts and disguises: Housman's

> They carry back bright to the coiner the mintage of man,
> The lads that will die in their glory and never grow old.

is curiously Elizabethan in its use of the adjective.

The line in *The Dream of Fair Women*,

> The bright death quivered at the victim's throat,

is paradoxical, a striking effect. Other examples of the general poetic idea stretch from Chaucer's Troilus—

> O paleis empty and disconsolat,
> O thou lantern of which queynt is the light,

and Spenser—

> The blazing brightness of her beauty's beam
> And glorious light of her sunshiny face,

down to T. S. Eliot's

> Weave, weave the sunlight in your hair.

Light, youth and pleasure are associated ideas.[1]

In Wordsworth we shall find the religious association clinging to such words as " light ", " radiant " and " shining ", which we have already glanced at in connection with " angel ". This he inherited with the mysticism of Vaughan and Traherne. Milton also is fond of the word " bright " in this connection: " The bright Seraphim ", " Winged Warriors bright ", " Bright squadrons ", " Bright aerial Spirits ", " Bright effluence of bright essence increate ".

But neither of these usages give the primary and original value of the word. There is no association of this kind in

> To pluck bright honour from the pale-faced moon,

or

> Put up your bright swords or the dew will rust them,

or

> Tyger! Tyger! Burning bright
> In the forests of the night,

or

> Ye have that bright bird in your bowers,

or

> But this lady is gone to her chamber,
> Her maidens following bright.

These last two quotations are from the Ballads.

[1] There is an attractive parallel usage of λαμπρός in the *Electra* of Sophocles. She believes that she holds the urn containing the ashes of her brother.

> νῦν μὲν γὰρ οὐδὲν ὄντα βαστάζω χεροῖν,
> δόμων δέ σ', ὦ παῖ, λαμπρὸν ἐξέπεμψ' ἐγώ.

The same contrast as in the quotations from the Elizabethan dramatists above.

Now adjectives in the Ballads are mainly conventional, such as "fair", "gay", "merry", or colour adjectives. But we have " My lady bright ", " armour bright ", " three sisters bright ", " Bright bride ", " the hawk with his bells sae bright " and " bright brown sword ". The reason for this is easily explained. The savage loves bright beads and polished metal, a baby clutches at anything bright and shining, from the firelight to a silver rattle. Thus *bright* has three values, one elementary, one symbolical, one of religious association. Chaucer has the elementary usage frequently; for instance: " fetheres brighte of Troy " and " lady brighte of hew ", " brighte thoughtes ", " eyen brighte ", " brighte teres ", " lufsome ladye brighte ", " brighte Goddes ". It is not surprising that the word, possessing these three values, occurs in the poets perpetually and effectively.

Golden has a similar but less subtle history, and has become more of a " gradus " epithet. It has the earliest association of ballads and nursery rhymes with kings and queens and golden crowns, and the association arising from the phrase " the golden age ", and lastly, the more sophisticated and by now sentimental association with youth of which *A Shropshire Lad* and the dirge in *Cymbeline* provide examples. How not to use such words as these, in fact how not to use adjectives, may be instanced by Wilde's stanza—

> All her bright golden hair,
> Tarnished with rust,
> She that was young and fair,
> Fallen to dust.

H

This is superficially pretty, but we are saved the trouble of thinking, and shall not therefore take the trouble to feel. *Bright* and *golden* damage each other, while either epithet tells us that she was young and fair. The second couplet feebly repeats the first, and melts like sugar in weak tea, when compared with the line in Donne, or the couplet in *Cymbeline*, which it echoes.

Golden is frequently an emotional adjective, a class which poets are inclined to exploit. *Little* is more emotional than *small*. Chaucer's " Litel son Lewis " touches the sentimentalist. Richard II. plays upon the word, " A little, little grave, an obscure grave ", and Marlowe's *Lascivious Queen*, " Bestow one smile, one little, little smile ". Keats has a weakness for it: " I stood tiptoe upon a little hill ", " A little noiseless noise among the leaves ". An ordinary unemotional adjective may be emotionally employed as in " I saw him go o'er the white Alps alone ", where " white " not only adds to the visual picture, but suggests " cold " and underlines " alone ". Or again, the words of Oenone:

> Hath he not sworn his love a thousand times,
> In this green valley under this green hill?

Green (of which we have spoken in a previous chapter) has a subtle value, recalling the young love Paris has betrayed. Valley and hill are green again, his faith is withered.[1] These undertones are by no means rare in poetry.

[1] In " 'a' babbled of green fields " the adjective has the same symbolical significance; the thoughts of the old sinner of Eastcheap return to his youth and salad days. The inevitability of the phrase is caused by the

Edmund Burke, according to a wit, envisaged the Sublime " as a grenadier with very large side-whiskers ". Certainly after reading *The Reflections*, the Beautiful appears as a soft, yielding, wayward creature, with tottering gait and a lisp in her speech, in fact what is tediously called " the Eternal feminine ". Yet even such a creature is superior to " That paralysing apparition, Beauty, the ineffable, ultimate, unanalysable, simple Idea " of aesthetic criticism, which Mr. Richards removes. " We are accustomed to say that a picture is beautiful, instead of saying that it causes an experience in us which is valuable in certain ways: . . . it is . . . a mere noise, signalling the fact that we approve of the picture. . . ." Now the poet is in a very different position to the art critic ; like Burke, he suggests the attributes of the Beautiful.

Though Mr. Richards bans the word " beautiful " in criticism, we shall find it and its synonyms often enough in poetry. When we say that a poem is beautiful, we may not only be signifying approval of the poem but indicating also the poet's subject. For ' beauty ' (that is the approval of a face, a sunset, or a cherry tree) is the commonest of poetic subjects. " I have loved the principle of beauty in all things ", wrote Keats

---

associative link which binds " babbled " (with its suggestion of brooks and running water) to " *green* fields ".

Note also the " placing " of the word in Blake:

" And did those feet in ancient time
Walk upon England's mountains green."

The two epithets contrast emphatically and symbolically.

in his Letters, and again: " I feel assured I should write for the mere yearning and fondness I have for the beautiful even if my night's labours should be burnt every morning, and no eye ever shine upon them ".

The poet has three methods of enchantment: by appealing to the five senses, by elaborate ornament or realistic detail, and by the use of general epithets synonymous with beautiful. By sensuous adjectives, I mean those which appeal to the eye and ear, the touch and taste and smell: *soft, tender, perfumed, bright, radiant, shining, sweet, silent, musical, cool.* ' *Sweet* ' links up the sensuous with the general epithet, such as *lovely, amorous, precious, fair, young, glorious* and *beautiful.* Poetry also favours among the synonyms of *beautiful* those of an intangible order, *frail, faint, dim, shadowy, pale, wan.* With occasional moments of detail and description, or naming flowers and gems and other objects upon which man has agreed to put a price as desirable, the poet is able to accumulate and combine not a few sensuous and general epithets and yet carry us with him.

A passage in *Christabel* supplies an excellent example of the poetic method.

> There she sees a damsel bright,
> Drest in a silken robe of white
> That shadowy in the moonlight shone.
> The neck that made the white robe wan,
> Her stately neck and arms were bare,
> Her blue-veined feet unsandalled were,
> And wildly glittered here and there
> The gems entangled in her hair.

Amid the general effect of shining light there is a moment of decorative detail and visual appeal:

Her blue-veined feet unsandalled were.

And the stanza lifts away with ease the conclusion and close:

Beautiful exceedingly.

The first paragraph of the *Song of the Lotos-Eaters* uses epithets in the same way—*sweet, softer, still, shadowy, gleaming, gentlier, sweet, cool*—and closes with detail, the long-leaved flowers in the stream and the poppy hanging from the craggy ledge.

Shelley prefers the general and intangible to the sensuous epithet. His eye never sees anything with a sharp outline, clear and complete; his world is " Beautiful as a wreck of Paradise ", faint and faded, peopled with grey phantoms and dim forms. Similarly Poe is lavish of such words as *dim, old, ultimate, far* and *shadowy*, while in the first stanza of *The Sleeper* he succeeds in piling one on top of the other, *mystic, opiate, dewy, dim, softly, quiet, drowsily, musically, steals, nods, lolls, softly dripping*, and then changes to a quicker motion, " O Lady bright, can it be right ". This is the real poetic diction. De la Mare follows Shelley and Poe in his choice of epithets. We find more detail in the Pre-Raphaelites, more sensuousness in Keats and the Elizabethans.

Many of these epithets are everyday words, the current coin of ordinary speech; but they are too simple, too essential to become commonplace and stale, which is the fate of more sophisticated words and

the fashionable terms of an age.   Poets depend upon
them: for instance—

> Modest as morn, as mid-day bright,
> Gentle as evening, cool as night,

or

> Sweet day, so calm and cool and bright.

While, in Cleopatra's death scene, after much fine
writing in the grand style, after " Give me my robe,
put on my crown . . . ", after

> Dissolve, thick cloud and rain, that I may say
> The gods themselves do weep. . . ,

comes the sudden relief of

> As sweet as balm, as soft as air, as gentle. . . ,

a line which dies away unfinished.

The shades and implications and histories of some
of the general epithets must now be considered more
minutely.

" Lovely " and " loveliness " are more frequent in
poetry (one might almost say more poetical, than
" beauty " and " beautiful "). A minor reason for
this is that the double ' L ' invites certain effects.

> Her gentle limbs did she undress
> And lay down in her loveliness.

Contrast this couplet from *Christabel* with one from
The Ancient Mariner—

> The many men so beautiful,
> And they all dead did lie,

and we realise that " lovely " is a far more personal
word (and therefore less suitable to the ballad manner of

The Ancient Mariner).   In fact, "lovely" preserves the
meanings of "amorous", "loving" and "lovable"
which it possesses in early literature.   Marlowe has
"lovely boys", Shakespeare "lovely Knights" and
A. E. Housman "lovely lads": in each case the word
has a slightly different meaning and implies more than
beautiful.   Housman also has "lovely muck" where
"beautiful" would be impossible.   Sidney's famous
phrase which Shelley echoes in *Adonais*—

> He is a portion of that loveliness
> Which once he made more lovely,

expresses truly one of the functions of poetry.   The
poet does not beautify but makes more dear.

"Beautiful" and "lovely" are rare in Milton, but
Eve wins the very words in which Othello addresses
Desdemona, "so lovely fair".   Of Eve also—

> Greatness of mind and nobleness their seat
> Build in her loveliest,

and "When I approach her loveliness . . .": the
Serpent at the moment of the temptation rightly shares
the honours of the word with Eve.

> Pleasing was his shape
> And lovely; never since of serpent kind
> Lovelier.

"Lovely" has, of course, Biblical association, which
is even more the case with "fair", the Miltonic
epithet *passim* for "beautiful", frequent in the ballads
and Elizabethans, now archaic and poetical (except in
the sense of "light-haired" or "light-complexioned"
or as an antithesis to "foul").   Biblical usages are

always worth studying in connection with Milton's
vocabulary; with him " fair " retains all the beauty it
has in the Song of Solomon (" fair as the moon ",
" fairest among women ", " How fair is thy love ",
" Rise up, my love, my fair one "), but it is also employed
as a noun (" the proud fair "), a common Restoration
usage, which (with the invention of the phrase " the
fair sex ") degraded the word.   Although poetry has
the advantage of prose, in that it is able to preserve
the best and primary meanings of words, " fair " has
to-day a faint suggestion of poetic diction and is most
effective among other slightly heightened words, as for
example in

> Never seraph spread a pinion
> Over fabric half so fair.

The Elizabethan epithet is not " beautiful ",
" lovely " or " fair ", although of course these all
occur, but " sweet ".   This is Shakespeare's favourite
adjective, his darling word, applied indiscriminately
(or so it seems to us) to all subjects.   In the sonnets
we find it in every other line: " sweet lip ", " sweet
ornament ", " sweet coral mouth ", " sweet kiss ",
" sweet desire ".   Besides the elementary and sensuous
use, the word means " lovely ", " dear ", " bitter sweet ":
here are some of the more curious uses—" sweet
chastity ", " sweet religion ", " sweet hay ", " sweet
thunder ", " sweet moonlight ".   Shakespeare is not
commonplace and conventional in his affection for the
word.   He has a weakness for the figure, oxymoron,
and exploits " sweet " subtly and effectively, to
intensify the emotional appeal: " Kneeling before

this ruin of sweet life ", " The sweet warman is dead
and rotten ", ". . . to seek sweet safety out in vaults
and prisons ", " Sweet soul, take heed, take heed of
perjury ", " Sweet bells jangled ", " sweet chastity's
decay ", " sweet Death ", " sweet uncleanness ". Sir
Philip Sidney has a happy oxymoron, " that sweet
enemy France ", a phrase which he culled from Bruno,
and Andrew Marvell perhaps borrowed it:

> To make a final conquest of all me
> Love did compose so sweet an enemy.

"Sweet" is everywhere in English poetry. Coleridge,
Keats and Shelley are Elizabethan in their preference
for it. But gradually the beauty of the word has begun
to wane, the enchantment to abate, and when we come
to Francis Thompson we may even find it sentimental.

> She knew not those sweet words she spake
> Nor knew her own sweet way,
> But there's never a bird so sweet a song
> Thronged in whose throat that day!

Be that as it may, it is surely significant that A. E.
Housman does not use the word at all in his poems.[1]

From the general poetical epithet, I shall turn now
to the decorative adjective and consider some of the
methods of particular poets. To begin at the beginning, the characteristics of the ballad are worth noticing.
As in Homer, the adjective is mainly conventional, the
result of oral tradition: milk-white steed, wan water,
lily hand, nut-brown maid, fair, bonny, gay, merry.

---

[1] *Sweet* is the epithet which the middle-aged Wordsworth pruned away
again and again from *The Prelude*.

The decoration is that of a children's picture book, because, after all, the appeal was to children. The adjectives are colour adjectives, bright and pleasant to the eye: red rose, red gold, red cock, green kirtle, green grass, green forest, green leaves; and

> The Queen was clad in scarlet,
> Her merry maids all in green,

and

> And clear, clear was her yellow hair
> Whereon the red blood drips.

Combined with these colours we find in the ballad the curious use of numbers:

> O we were sisters, sisters seven.

> There were three ravens sat on a tree.

> O gin my sons were seven rats.

> Four and twenty ladies fair
> Were playing at the chess.

> At ilka tett o' her horse's mane
> Hung fifty siller bells and nine;

and the nine nurses,

> Three to sleep and three to wake
> And three to go between.

The effect is flat and impersonal: the knights and ladies are marshalled before us as in a tapestry.

The conventional and yet unsophisticated epithet, which is so marked a feature of the ballad, attracted William Morris, who scattered colour adjectives among the lyrics of *The Defence of Guenevere* volume, like a child with a paint-box. Scarlet sleeves and lilies, blue flowers and purple beds, catch the eye, and one poem particularly, *Golden Wings*, with its numerous repetitions and intertwining strands of colour, is at once rich in effect and curiously simple; red roofs, red apples, red rust, red lips, red morning sun; yellow lichen, yellow sand; green moss, green hangings, green water, green lawn; scarlet bricks, scarlet shoon; painted drawbridge, painted wood, blue eyes, blue painted boat. This is unique, and, I think, perfectly successful, although opinion may differ as to how far it is worth doing.

But repetition is a far more usual device in poetry than the ordinary reader imagines. Not only are certain words, as we have seen, the current coin of poetry, whose stamp becomes very little defaced by time, but also the same word often appears and re-appears several times in a single poem or passage, in what seems a very uninventive way. Thus in the last paragraph of *Sohrab and Rustum* " bright " occurs three times; or take some fifty lines from *The Merchant of Venice*, Act V. Scene 1:

Sweet soul, let's in and there expect their coming . . .	l. 49
How sweet the moonlight sleeps upon this bank . . .	53
. . . soft stillness and the night	
Becomes the touches of sweet harmony.	57
With sweetest touches pierce your mistress' ear . . .	67
I am never merry when I hear sweet music . . .	69
Their savage eyes turned to a modest gaze	
By the sweet power of music . . .	79
The man that hath no music in himself	
Nor is not moved by concord of sweet sounds . . .	84
Methinks it sounds much sweeter than by day . . .	100
The crow doth sing as sweetly as the lark	103
When neither is attended . . .	

This is indeed " linked sweetness long drawn out ".
Poetry is simple and sensuous, not complex and
sophisticated, and the poet plays upon a single emotion
and moves us by his insistence upon one single note.
More remarkable still, under analysis, is the use of
words in *The Ancient Mariner*.   Here Coleridge has
elaborated the devices of the ballad, until the ring of
the phrases is now like the chime, now like the toll of
a bell.   The adjectives catch each other up at unexpected moments.   Thus " the bright-eyed mariner "
(twice) is taken up immediately by " The sun shone
bright "; again " the broad, bright sun " (Part III),
and " the hornéd moon with one bright star ", and in
Part IV.:

> The ocean hath no blast,
> His great bright eye most silently
> Up to the moon is cast.

This is followed by " The rock shone bright, the kirk
no less ", and we return finally to " The Mariner whose
eye is bright ".   Similarly " soft ", " strange ",
" swift " and " silent " echo each other from verse to
verse, and " sweet " also occurs some seven times.
" Shadow ", a word of great poetic power (which
springs partly from the association with darkness and
death, partly from the suggestion of " phantom ", the
effect being much enhanced by the " sh " sound), is
cunningly repeated as follows:

> As who pursued with yell and blow
> Still treads the shadow of his foe
> And forward bends his head.

> But where the ship's huge shadow lay
> The charméd water burnt alway
> A still and awful red.
>
> Beyond the shadow of the ship
> I watched the water snakes.
>
> And on the bay the moonlight lay
> And the shadow of the moon;

and only a stanza later:

> Full many shapes that shadows were
> In crimson colours came.
>
> A little distance from the prow
> Their crimson shadows were.

Through the darkness glimmers the fog-smoke white, the white moonshine, the white gleam of the steersman's face, the white foam, the white silent bay, the tracks of shining white. One shivers at this Apocalyptic vision of bright light and black shadows, which is shot with lurid colours, so different in effect from those of Morris—the ice green as emerald, the bloody sun, the water burning, blue and green and white, like a witch's oils, or a still and awful red, the rich attire of the water snakes.

> Blue, glossy green and velvet black.

Nowhere else in poetry are the elements so powerfully presented, except in *Macbeth*. And as there the grim horror of that atmosphere of murk and blood is intensified and thrown into relief by Banquo's speech about the temple-haunting martlet, so here while the Mariner unfolds his tale of agony, we know that

> In the garden bower the bride
> And bride-maids singing are.

The study of repetition has caused us to retrace our steps to the familiar adjectives, " bright " and " sweet ", which, like Simon Lee, have to bear a weighty burden of years upon their backs. We must turn now to those poets who gain their effects by variety and accumulation of adjectives. Keats found language inadequate. " I know not how to express my devotion ", he wrote to Fanny Brawne. " I want a brighter word than bright, a fairer word than fair." To express his devotion to poetry he squandered all the treasures of his Elizabethan vocabulary or hypnotised himself with the deliberate repetition of a single word.

> 'Tis not through envy of thy happy lot
> But being too happy in thy happiness.
>
> Ah happy, happy boughs! that cannot shed
>   Your leaves nor ever bid the spring adieu,
> And, happy melodist, unwearied
>   For ever piping songs for ever new.
> More happy love! more happy, happy love,
>   For ever warm and still to be enjoyed. . . .
>
> But who wast thou, O happy, happy dove?

His usual method is that of Marlowe and of Swinburne, to scatter epithets pell-mell, delighting the sense and the eye without stimulating the imagination. Any ten lines of *Endymion* offer a good example.

>   O thou, to whom
> Broad-leavéd fig-trees even now foredoom
> Their ripened fruitage; yellow-girted bees
> Their golden honeycombs; our village leas
> Their fairest-blossomed beans and poppied corn ;
> The chuckling linnet its five young unborn,

> To sing for thee; low, creeping strawberries
> Their summer coolness; pent-up butterflies
> Their freckled wings; yea, the fresh-budding year
> All its completions. . . .

In the fragmentary *Ode to Maia* and in the *Ode to Autumn*, Keats has his epithets well under control; he does not strangle his substantives with scarves of silk and smother his verbs with the down of phoenixes. In *Hyperion* we have something to bite on; the run honey of *Endymion* flows from the Miltonic comb. But the Miltonic epithet and arrangement of epithets were alien to Keats. They repay careful study.

In *Paradise Regained* Milton speaks of Greek poetry thus:

> Remove their swelling epithets, thick-laid
> As varnish on a harlot's cheek, the rest
> Thin-sown with aught of profit or delight.

The answer is "Thou art the man". Milton's earlier self stands condemned. In *Comus*, in the *Ode on the Nativity*, the epithets are swelling and thick-laid indeed; blossoms dressed and trained, but plentiful, not lopped and pruned as in his later style. No less plentiful than in Keats, their positions are infinitely varied; they are selected with the utmost subtlety and care. The first and most natural arrangement is this:

> The loose train of thy amber-dropping hair.   (*a b a b*)

> Through the soft silence of the listening night.

> Lest our frail thoughts dally with false surmise.

Secondly, the reverse of that:

> Ye myrtles brown with ivy never sere.   (*b a b a*)
>
> Of turkis blue and emerald green.
>
> In service high and anthems clear.

The third variation is:

> The star-led wizards haste with odours sweet.   (*a b b a*)
>
> Russet lawns and fallows grey.
>
> In dismal dance about the furnace blue.
>
> While the still morn went out with sandals grey.

This also may be reversed:

> Hence with denial vain and coy excuse.   (*b a a b*)
>
> Hymns devout and holy psalms.
>
> Not Typhon huge ending in snaky twine.
>
> And cowslips wan that hang the pensive head.

Very favourite and effective is the sandwiched noun:
" branching elm star-proof ", " Alpine mountains
cold ", " forc'd fingers rude ", " cany waggons light ",
" beckoning shadows dire ", " timbrel'd anthems
dark ", " storied windows richly dight ", " jealous leer
malign ", " unblessed enchanter vile ".   One line not
seldom carries three adjectives in various positions:

> Infamous hills and sandy perilous wilds.
>
> In regions mild of calm and serene air.
>
> Bitter constraint and sad occasion dear.
>
> Of noisome winds and blasting vapours chill.

The advantages of this artificial juggling are manifold
and apparent. New contrasts, new harmonies, new

emphases are suggested. Such high light is thrown
upon the epithet that it cannot afford to be conventional
or insignificant. Each one stands on equal terms with
the noun and must justify its existence and artificial
setting. Consequently a great strain is put upon the
ingenuity and invention of the poet; but if he moves
slowly, he will at least avoid being slovenly and escape
the accusation of padding his verses. In Milton the
epithet is either highly decorative or else unfamiliar in
its form or application. Sometimes following classical
precedent, sometimes with the Elizabethans (particularly Shakespeare) as his guide, he distils into the
double epithet all the colour and romance he can. In
his earlier poetry we find among others: " yellow-
skirted ", " silver - buskined ", " flowre - inwoven ",
" rosie - bosomed ", " vermeil - tinctured ", " tinsel -
slippered ", " dew - besprent ", " dewy - feathered ",
" amber-dropping ", " grey-hooded ", " sable-stoled ",
" rushy - fringed ", " flowery - kirtled ". His single
epithets take one by surprise either in themselves or
in their context; for example, " speckled vanity ",
" melodious tear ", " tawny sands ", " amorous clouds "
" leprous sin ", " monumental oak ", " uncouth cell ",
" stoic fur ". They puzzle and distress the superficial
reader. Shakespeare and Keats have their " bookish "
adjectives although in a lesser degree than Milton;
where he really differs from them is in his very sparing
use of sensuous words. Instead he has a peculiar fondness for epithets which are best described as " urban ".
I am thinking of " pert ", " spruce ", " trim ", " coy ",
" nice ", " sleek ", " mincing ", " gaudy ", " dapper ",

" trickt and frounced ", " spangled ", " debonair ",
by means of which he turns his nymphs, goddesses and
fairies into misses of the Restoration court. This
trait in his poetry is curious and not wholly pleasing.
Keats's Cockney errors in taste are well known and
unimportant, but one wonders whether Milton, however Puritanical about "the adulteries of art", preferred "the proud fair " and the Muse (the reason
may be literary, it may be personal)

> Still to be neat, still to be drest
> As you were going to a feast.

Even before he divested himself of the rich embroidery of his earlier poems his affinity was with
Horace (witness the *Sonnets*) rather than with Keats.
Endymion may blossom like a rose, but it remains a
wilderness: Milton's flowers never grew outside the
walls and ornamental beds of a garden, although
" sweeter than i' th' open field ".

There is nothing more absorbing than a study of
the Milton manuscripts in Trinity College Library;
in following the erasures and revisions one's sense
of word values is sharpened. The ode *At a
Solemn Music* has many important changes, which
centre round the epithet. Four lines are cut out
altogether:

> and as your equal raptures temper'd sweet
> in high mysterious *holy* spousal meet   happy
> snatch us from earth awhile
> us of our selves and *home-bred* woes beguile.   native

The earlier version has " fresh green " palms altered
to " blooming " and then finally to " victorious ".

" The youthful Cherubim, sweet-winged squires . . . Heaven's henchmen " become the more sedate "Cherubick host in thousand quires ". " Whilst the whole frame of Heaven and arches blue resound and echo Hallelu " turns into " all the starry rounds and arches blue " and then disappears. The decorative and the emotional adjective, the Elizabethan *sweet* and *sweet-winged*, were out of harmony with the simplicity and severity of the poem. Milton selected epithets here for their actual meaning, even more for their sound values.

Modern poets have a difficult task; most adjectives have become conventionalised or recall some famous context. It is not surprising that thay have to go far afield; unfortunately one cannot always say, as Johnson said of the conceits of the Metaphysicals, that their adjectives are worth the carriage. The Sitwells experiment in a sort of sleight-of-hand; that is, they interchange the senses, expressing the visible in terms of the audible, translating an experience of the ear or eye into one of the touch and smell. Miss Sitwell explains the phrase " creaking light ", for instance, as follows: ". . . in a very early dawn, after rain, the light has a curious uncertain quality, as though it does not run quite smoothly. Also, it falls in hard cubes, squares and triangles, which, again, give one the impression of a creaking sound, because of the association with wood." Later in the same poem the epithet *whining* is applied, because " the shivering movement of a certain cold dawn light upon the floor suggests a kind of high animal whining or whimpering, a kind of half-frightened and subservient urge to something outside our consciousness ". This is convincing, but can such poems be read without a commentary? The poet wagers the value of individual associations at first hand against the emotional value of general and universal associations.

The poet's orbit lies indeed behind these two poles of desire; the desire to appeal to the old instincts and the desire to take us by surprise. The new word challenges the old, the present is matched against the past, the freshness of the debutante, as it were, against the beauty of " an autumnal face ". Every word has its history and character and is particular about the company it keeps. And the poet well acquainted with many, on terms of friendship with not a few, selects those which will both have something in common and display each other at their best. But words, like human beings, have a weakness for cliques and coteries and these a new poet breaks down, seeking new elements, new combinations; or he may turn aside and, in the spell of a name, clutch for a moment the inviolable shade.

I have attempted to put down a few ideas and conclusions of my own on the behaviour of words and the conduct of poets, with the hope, even the belief, that some one may be induced thereby not only to analyse but also to *synthesise* their experiences in poetry, and by probing below the surface in the examination of word-values, may attain to a more rational and a more intense enjoyment. There comes a time when the disciple quite suddenly feels that he has grasped, has come to grips with, something in literature, has caught a glimpse of the mechanism of poetry from reading and writing it (I quote my own case), and rushes into the market-place to prophesy; where he is left post, whistling to the air.

The main difference between prose and poetry is that which distinguishes sculpture and painting. Prose, like sculpture, is confined by a certain actuality, created in a third dimension: but the painter suggests more than he can represent.

PART II

NOTES AND QUOTATIONS PREPARATORY TO A STUDY OF SHAKESPEARE'S DICTION AND STYLE

I

INFLUENCE AND IMITATION

Whenever you write, say a word or two on some passage in Shakespeare that may have come rather new to you, which must be continually happening, notwithstanding that we read the same play forty times.—*Keats's Letters,* 18*th* April 1817.

SHAKESPEARE, ONE FEELS, after perusing the two volumes devoted to him in the British Museum catalogue, has fallen like his own Hero into a pit of ink. The wide sea hath drops too few to wash him clean again. He has been brought before the inquisition of posterity as man, poet, dramatist, husband, lover, sailor, actor, Christian; and had to abide questions upon his morals, family, handwriting and versification. One subject alone has curiously escaped notice—his style. There are a few just generalisations, stray papers and occasional essays; analyses, from Johnson and Coleridge down to Saintsbury and Kellett. But the rest is silence—or a chorus of praise. The subject has never really been faced. The student has two crutches to aid him: Schmidt's Lexicon and the more or less reliable chronology of the plays based upon external evidence and versification tests. The second enables him wise after the event to trace changes and developments in the use of words.

The following notes are the fruit of my own reading; they are not pilfered from the commentaries of annotated editions. I am fully aware that many of the parallels quoted must have been remarked before, but I know no book in which they have been collected and arranged in an illuminating way.

Shakespeare's sensibility to words is often betrayed, critically, in an aside or an allusion or a comment from one of his clowns. Such sensibility is, after all, the *sine qua non* of a poet and would be all the more keen and alert at a time when language was fermenting and, as it were, coming to the boil; when every poetaster was experimenting, stirring, flavouring; every new dish became the rage, every fashion was carried to an extreme.

Two superstitions must be cleared up. The first is that Shakespeare, because he never blotted a line and wrote *The Merry Wives* in a fortnight, took no more thought for his vocabulary and style than the lilies of the field for their raiment. Shakespeare varies. Sometimes he is scribbling, sometimes he is scratching his head, sometimes he is " cribbing ", or versifying his authorities. Now he has his eye on the clock, and now on the stars and eternity. In the earlier plays, especially the histories, the unevenness of the style, the uncertainty of the creative force, is made apparent in the different speeds of the lines and paragraphs. Now and again a couplet occurs in which Shakespeare has lingered to blow away the dust and give a final polish:

> O death, made proud with pure and princely beauty,
> The earth had not a hole to hide this deed.

> Life is as tedious as a twice-told tale
> Vexing the dull ear of a drowsy man.

> The sly slow hours shall not determinate
> The dateless limit of thy dear exile.

> The milk thou suck'st from her did turn to marble,
> Even at thy teat thou hadst thy tyranny.

There is selection here and arrangement; they stand out stylistically from their contexts.

The second superstition or fallacy lies in the belief that all the Elizabethans wrote the same language. Elizabethan Poetic Diction, with reference to Shakespeare, is a subject which I hope, after more reading, to undertake. Shakespeare has all the tricks and clichés of the time, but he developed a completely individual style and possessed an individual vocabulary. He is often as weak, and usually more obscure, more condensed, than any of them, but he is always unlike. The same symbols and imagery, the same prettiness, the same sublime can be instanced in all the playwrights, but if we examine their phrases, their use of adjectives, their word preferences, the main figures are only less unlike each other than they are to Shakespeare. His apprenticeship was long, his development gradual, his final style difficult and unique. But that final style has birth-marks, as it were, signs and echoes of his previous work, even as that echoes and imitates the literature of the time.

Shakespeare's earlier manner (before 1600, roughly) is partly imitative, partly hackwork and plagiarism, partly Shakespearian. For the moment it is with the imitative part that I am concerned. In these first plays he is speaking the Elizabethan language rather than his own, flirting with new fashions and seduced by the poetic diction of the day. The following quotations are selected and arranged with the idea of linking certain plays to each other and to the earlier sonnets, of suggesting some relation with Spenser, and of emphasising the frequent use of conventional imagery.

The artificial descriptions of the sun and sunrise, classical in origin, provide good examples. Chaucer had little leisure or taste for descriptive fancy, but these lines in *The Knight's Tale* are important:

> The busy larke, messenger of day,
> Salueth in hir song the morwe gray
> And firy Phebus riseth up so brighte
> That all the orient laugheth of the light,
> And with his stremes dryeth in the greves
> The silver dropes, hangynge on the leves.

Juliet says—

> It was the lark, the herald of the morn,

and Troilus—

> O Cressida, but that the busy day
> Waked by the lark.

Not an imitation, hardly a memory, but in the same tradition.

Phoebus, on the other hand, fathers numerous offspring.

From Spenser:

> At last the golden Oriental gate
> Of greatest heaven gan to open fair,
> And Phoebus fresh as bridegroom to his mate
> Came dancing forth shaking his deawie hair;

Henry VI. Pt. 3:

> See how the morning opes her golden gates,
> And takes her farewell of the glorious sun.
> How well resembles it the prime of youth,
> Trimm'd like a younker prancing to his love,

which has a link with the sonnets:

> Lo! in the orient when the gracious light
> Lifts up his burning head . . .
> And having climbed the steep-up heavenly hill
> Resembling strong youth in his middle age.

From Spenser again:

> Scarcely had Phoebus in the glooming east
> Yet harnessed his fiery-footed team.

> Phoebus fiery car
> In haste was climbing up the Eastern hill,
> Full envious that night so long his room did fill.

> And now fair Phoebus gan decline in haste
> His weary waggon to the western vale.

> And Titan playing on the eastern streams
> Gan clear the dewy air with springing light.

> Her looks were like beams of the morning sun
> Forth looking through the windows of the east.

Shakespeare has the following similar but more pictorial passages—two are from the sonnets, the rest from the plays, showing a like style throughout.

> As when the golden sun salutes the morn,
> And having gilt the ocean with his beams,
> Gallops the zodiac in his glistering coach,
> And overlooks the highest-peering hills.
>
> (*Titus Andronicus.*)

As doth the blushing discontented sun
From out the fiery portal of the east;
When he perceives the envious clouds are bent
To dim his glory and to stain the track
Of his bright passage to the occident.   (*Richard II.*)

Full many a glorious morning have I seen
Flatter the mountain tops with sovereign eye,
Kissing with golden face the meadows green,
Gilding pale streams with heavenly alchymy.   (*Sonnets.*)

                    the glorious sun
Stays in his course and plays the alchemist
Turning with splendour of his precious eye
The meagre cloddy earth to glittering gold.
                                    (*King John.*)

As plays the sun upon the glassy streams.
                                (*2 Henry VI.*)

                an hour before the worshipped sun
Peer'd forth the golden window of the east.
                            (*Romeo and Juliet.*)

At the first opening of the gorgeous east.
                            (*Love's Labour's Lost.*)

        Look, love, what envious streaks
Do lace the severing clouds in yonder east:
Night's candles are burnt out, and jocund day
Stands tiptoe on the misty mountain tops.
                            (*Romeo and Juliet.*)

            not so bright
As those gold candles fixed in heaven's air.   (*Sonnets.*)

        The silent hours steal on
And flaky darkness breaks within the east.   (*Richard III.*)

The grey-eyed morn smiles on the frowning night,
Chequering the eastern clouds with streaks of light,
And flecked darkness like a drunkard reels
From forth day's path and Titan's fiery wheels.
                            (*Romeo and Juliet.*)

Almost the last example of this objective decorative manner is to be found in *Hamlet*.

> But, look, the morn in russet mantle clad
> Walks o'er the dew of yon high eastern hill.

This is the work of the poet and prentice, not of the dramatist; richer in effect than Spenser, who never achieved such a condensed and telling line as—

> He fires the proud tops of the eastern pines.
>
> *(Richard II.)*

Marston treats the same theme with more elaboration and prettiness:

> Is not yon gleam the shuddering morn that flakes
> With silver tincture the east verge of heaven?

> For see the dapple-grey coursers of the morn
> Beat up the light with their bright silver hooves
> And chase it through the sky.

But he is hardly more poetical than Don Pedro:

> Good morrow, masters: put your torches out:
>   The wolves have preyed and look, the gentle day,
> Before the wheels of Phoebus, round about
>   Dapples the drowsy east with spots of grey.

A notable characteristic of the diction of the Sonnets is the naming of the seasons, usually with a metaphorical significance: Spenser again provides suggestive parallels, and the links between the sonnets and the early plays are even closer.

> Such rage as winters, reigneth in my heart,
> My life blood friesing with unkindly cold:
> Such stormy stoures do breed my baleful smart,
> As if my year were waste and waxen old.

All so my lustful leafe is drye and sere,
My timely buds with wailing all are wasted:
The blossome, which my branch of youth did beare,
With breathed sighs is blown away and blasted,
And from mine eyes the drizling tears descend
As on your boughs the ysicles depend.

(Shep. Kal., Jan.)

And careful hours with Time's deformed hand
Have written strange defeatures in my face. . . .
Though now this grained face of mine be hid
In sap-consuming winter's drizzled snow.

(Comedy of Errors.)

How like a winter hath my absence been
From thee, the pleasure of the fleeting year!
What freezings have I felt, what dark days seen!
What old December's bareness everywhere!

(Sonnets.)

So now my year drawes to his latter terme,
My spring is spent, my sommer burnt up quite:
My harvest hastes to stirre up winter sterne,
And bids him claim with rigorous rage his right.

The careful cold hath nypt my rugged rynde,
And in my face deep furrowes eld hath pight:
My head besprent with hoary frost I find,
And by myne eie the crowe his claw dooth wright.

(Shep. Kal., Dec.)

For never-resting time leads summer on
To hideous winter, and confounds him there;
Sap check'd with frost and lusty leaves quite gone,
Beauty o'ersnowed and bareness everywhere.

(Sonnets.)

And after summer evermore succeeds
Barren winter with his wrathful nipping cold.

(2 Henry VI.)

For far more bitter storm than winters stowre
The beauty of the world hath lately wasted,
And those fresh buds which wont so faire to flowre,
Hath marred quite and all their blossoms blasted:
And those young plants which wont with fruit t' abound,
Now without fruit or leaves are to be found.

(Tears of the Muses.)

Thus are my blossoms blasted in the bud
And caterpillars eat my leaves away.   (2 Henry VI.)

Death lies on her like an untimely frost
Upon the sweetest flower of all the field.

(Romeo and Juliet.)

His summer leaves all vaded.

For that same goodly hue of white and red
With which the cheeks are sprinckled, shal decay,
And those sweet rosy leaves so fairly spred,
Upon the lips shall fade and fall away.

(Hymne in Honour of Beauty.)

The air hath starved the roses in her cheeks
And pinched the lily-tincture of her face.

(Two Gentlemen.)

The roses in thy lips and cheeks shall fade
To paly ashes.   (Romeo and Juliet.)

Then let not winter's ragged hand deface
In thee thy summer, ere thou be distilled.   (Sonnets.)

But earthlier happy is the rose distilled
Than that which withering on the virgin thorn
Grows, lives and dies in single blessedness.

(Midsummer Night's Dream.)

Of pure complexions, that shall quickly fade
And passe away like to a summer's shade.

(Spenser's Hymne.)

But thy eternal summer shall not fade.   (Sonnets.)

Disdain to root the summer-swelling flower
And make rough winter everlastingly.   (Two Gentlemen.)

K

Time with his sickle, the rose and the canker, are common in Spenser as they are in the *Sonnets*. Here are some further examples of Shakespeare's poetic manner in the earlier plays in this connection:

> as in the sweetest bud
> The eating canker dwells, so eating love
> Inhabits in the finest wits of all.   (*Two Gentlemen.*)

> This canker that eats up Love's tender spring.
>   (*Venus and Adonis.*)

> For canker vice the sweetest buds doth love.

> And loathsome canker lives in sweetest bud.   (*Sonnets.*)

> But now will canker sorrow eat my bud
> And chase the native beauty from his cheek.   (*King John.*)

> As is the bud bit by the envious worm,
> Ere he can spread his sweet leaves to the air,
> Or dedicate his beauty to the sun.   (*Romeo and Juliet.*)

> an envious sneaping frost
> That bites the first-born infants of the spring.
>   (*Love's Labour's Lost.*)

> Like little frosts that sometimes threat the spring,
> To add a more rejoicing to the prime,
> And give the sneaped birds more cause to sing.   (*Lucrece.*)

> Their lips were four red roses on a stalk,
> Which in their summer beauty kissed each other . . .
> The most replenished sweet work of nature
> That from the prime creation e'er she framed.
>   (*Richard III.*)

> Such comfort as do lusty young men feel
> When well-apparel'd April on the heel
> Of limping winter treads.   (*Romeo and Juliet.*)

> When proud-pied April, dressed in all his trim,
> Hath put a spirit of youth in every thing,
> That heavy Saturn laughed and leaped with him. (*Sonnets.*)

Two other couplets, one from *The Two Gentlemen of Verona*, the second from *King John*, would more naturally be ascribed to the *Sonnets*: in the first substitute *thine* for *mine* to make it even more clear.

> Omitting the sweet benefit of time
> To clothe mine age with angel-like perfection.

> But thou art fair; and at thy birth, dear boy,
> Nature and Fortune joined to make thee great:
> Of Nature's gifts thou may'st with lilies boast
> And with the half-blown rose.

The argument of *Venus and Adonis* is the argument of the third book of *The Faërie Queene*.

> Seeds spring from seeds, and beauty breedeth beauty,
> Thou wast begot; to get it is thy duty.

And the entreaties of Venus are echoed again in the first seventeen sonnets:

> And nothing 'gainst Time's scythe can make defence
> Save breed.

Milton in *Comus* repeats in the Elizabethan manner the same Elizabethan theme:

> If you let slip time, like a neglected rose
> It withers on the stalk with languished head.

> Make use of time, let not advantage slip,
> Beauty within itself should not be wasted.
>
> *(Venus and Adonis.)*

The familiar imagery and conceits of crystal and pearl and tears, the artificial descriptions—" ruby-coloured portal ", " breasts like ivory globes ", " azure veins, coral lips, alabaster skin "—are as abundant in the

poems, as in Spenser and the earlier Elizabethans.
The sonnets draw their imagery from flowers more
than from precious stones.   The plays have instances.

> A sea of melting pearl which some call tears.
>
> *(Two Gentlemen.)*

> Ah, but those tears are pearl which thy love sheds.
>
> *(Sonnets.)*

> And that same dew, which sometimes on the buds
> Was wont to swell like round and orient pearls,
> Stood now within the pretty flowerets' eyes
> Like tears that did their own disgrace bewail.
>
> *(Midsummer Night's Dream.)*

Shakespeare in his later work discarded this external
ornament and turned his conceits into links knitting
his speeches more closely together.

After Spenser—Marlowe and the university wits.
What influence had they on Shakespeare?   He is less
sensuous and less educated.   He does not rifle the
Metamorphoses of Ovid, as do Marlowe and Greene.
Titus Andronicus and *Richard III.* and *Richard II.*
are partly imitative in their different ways of the
Seneca-Marlowe-Kyd school.   Spenser affected Shakespeare's purely poetic manner, Marlowe to a lesser
extent his rhetorical and dramatic style.   Here are
some examples:

> Then Aaron, arm thy heart, and fit thy thoughts
> To mount aloft with thy imperial mistress,
> And mount her pitch, whom thou in triumph long
> Hast prisoner held fettered in amorous chains,
> And faster bound to Aaron's charming eyes
> Than is Prometheus tied to Caucasus.
> Away with slavish weeds and servile thoughts!

I will be bright, and shine in pearl and gold,
To wait upon this new-made empress.
To wait, said I?   To wanton with this queen,
This goddess, this Semiramis, this nymph.

Titus shows the love of names characteristic of the school
— Pyramus, Tereus, Enceladus, Tarquin, Alcides,
Hecuba, Acheron, Pluto.   In these young men, devour-
ing books and discovering the classical mythology,
literature bred literature, as afterwards in Keats and
Beddoes and Swinburne.

Single you hither then this dainty doe.
>   (*Titus.*   Cf. Peele's " roe ")

How sweet a thing it is to wear a crown;
Within whose circuit is Elysium
And all that poets feign of bliss and joy.   (3 *Henry VI.*)

Speak, gentle niece, what stern ungentle hands
Have lopped and hewed and made thy body bare
Of her two branches, those sweet ornaments
Whose circling shadows kings have sought to sleep in.
>   (*Titus.*)

Streaming the ensign of the Christian cross.   (*Richard II.*)

Sluiced out his innocent soul through streams of blood.
>   (*Richard II.*)

The precious image of our dear Redeemer.   (*Richard III.*)

I tell thee, Pole, when in the city Tours
Thou ran'st a tilt in honour of my love
And stol'st away the ladies' hearts of France,
I thought King Henry had resembled thee.

>   (2 *Henry VI.*)

Oh that I were a mockery king of snow,
To melt myself away in waterdrops.

>   (*Richard II.*)

Why, Phaethon——for thou art Merops' son——
Wilt thou aspire to guide the heavenly car
And with thy daring folly burn the world?

(*Two Gentlemen.*)

like glistering Phaethon
Wanting the manage of unruly jades. (*Richard II.*)

Gallop apace, you fiery-footed steeds,
Towards Phoebus' lodging: such a waggoner
As Phaethon would whip you to the west,
And bring in cloudy night immediately.

(*Romeo and Juliet.*)

The movement and manner of these last three differ subtly from the sunrise descriptions already noted.

And breathed such life with kisses in my lips
That I revived and was an emperor.

(*Romeo and Juliet.*)

From the four corners of the earth they come,
To kiss this shrine, this mortal-breathing saint;
The Hyrcanian deserts and the vasty wilds
Of wide Arabia are as throughfares now
For princes to come view fair Portia:
The watery kingdom, whose ambitious head
Spits in the face of heaven, is no bar
To stop the foreign spirits, but they come,
As o'er a brook, to see fair Portia.

(*Merchant of Venice.*)

The Zenocrate refrain inspired many; for instance, one on Angelica in Greene's *Orlando Furioso*. Shakespeare strikes the same note for a moment.

II

THE EARLY SHAKESPEARIAN MANNER

MORTON LUCE finds the *Lucrece* far inferior to the *Venus and Adonis*. " We have less nature, less melody, less beauty, less poetry than in the earlier poem." The answer is that we have more Shakespeare, more of the dramatic poet. He himself promises in his dedication of the first poem that the second is to be " some graver labour ".

Ornament in the *Venus and Adonis* is supplied by similes. The bird tangled in the net, the dive-dapper peering through a wave, the shooting star, the night-wanderer, the snail with tender horn, the nurse's song, seem to belong to a more natural world. The shrill-tongued tapsters, the breeding jennet (taken from Du Bartas),

> What recketh he his rider's angry stir,
> His flattering " Holla " or his " Stand, I say " ?

and poor Wat, the hunted hare, even if academic imitations, are free and simple in spirit and style. Delightful and individual is the little cry with which Shakespeare introduces his decoration.

> Lo, here the gentle lark, weary of rest.
>
> Look, when a painter would surpass the life.
>
> Look, how a bright star shooteth from the sky.
>
> But lo, from forth a copse that neighbours by.

Lucrece is dramatic. Shakespeare is striving to realise the sensations of the two protagonists. There is a conflict in Tarquin before the rape, similar to that in the heart of Macbeth—

> But as he is my kinsman, my dear friend,
> The shame and fault finds no excuse or end.
>
> *(Lucrece, 237.)*

> He's here in double trust;
> First, as I am his kinsman and his subject;
>
> *(Macbeth, I. 7.)*

and to Brutus's " insurrection in the state of man "—

> Between the acting of a dreadful thing
> And the first motion.

Again when Tarquin prays that the heavens may countenance his sin, he starts reflecting—

> The powers to whom I pray abhor this fact,
> How can they then assist me in the act?

and he is in the same position as Claudius—

> O what form of prayer
> Can serve my turn?

Dramatically imaginative is the meeting between Lucrece and her maid; even more so her misinterpretation of the " homely villein's " bashful blushes as consciousness of her shame.

In this piece poetry gives place to rhetoric, simile to metaphor, description to soliloquy, Spenserian imagery to euphuistic, antithetical conceits. The metaphors are pursued laboriously and at length in a way which is very characteristic of Shakespeare's early manner; for although *Lucrece* is more dramatic, the plays, especially (and naturally so) the chronicle plays, suffer stylistically from their narrative qualities.

Here the metaphorical idea of an army setting siege to a city, which is found elsewhere in Shakespeare and the Elizabethans, for example—

> She will not stay the siege of loving terms
> Nor bide the encounter of assailing eyes.
> *(Romeo and Juliet.)*

is elaborated over eight stanzas (427-483). Here also the familiar conceits upon " windy sighs ", " the ocean of tears beating on the rocky heart ", which are to be found even in the final plays. *Lucrece*, weighty, prest, obstructive, contains most of the material, the superstitions, saws, fables and unnatural history, out of which *Henry VI., Richard III.* and *II.*, and *Romeo and Juliet* are composed.

> Nor read the subtle-shining secrecies
> Writ in the glassy margents of such books.
> *(Lucrece.)*

> And what obscured in this fair volume lies
> Find written in the margent of his eyes.
> *(Romeo and Juliet.)*

> Mud not the fountain that gave drink to thee.
> *(Lucrece, three uses.)*

> The purest spring is not so free from mud
> As I am clear from treason to my sovereign.
> *(2 Henry VI.)*

> Roses have thorns and silver fountains mud.
> *(Sonnets.)*

> Thou sheer, immaculate and silver fountain,
> From whence the stream through muddy passages
> Hath held his current and defiled himself.
> *(Richard II.)*

The proverbial instance is elaborated, as often.

> And now this pale swan in her watery nest
> Begins the sad dirge of her certain ending.   (*Lucrece*.)

> I am the cygnet to this pale faint swan,
> Who chants a doleful hymn to his own death.
>
>   (*King John*.)

> The face, that map which deep impression bears
> Of hard misfortune.   (*Lucrece*.)

> I see as in a map the end of all.   (*Richard III*.)

>   In thy face I see
> The map of honour, truth and loyalty.   (*2 Henry VI*.)

> Thus is his cheek the map of days outworn.   (*Sonnets*.)

> Poor broken glass, I often did behold
> In thy sweet semblance my old age new born.
>
>   (*Lucrece*.)

> Thou art thy mother's glass and she in thee
> Calls back the lovely April of her prime.   (*Sonnets*.)

Lucrece has the seeds of the history plays—the few examples above could be multiplied. The style is dense and cumbersome, a cloak worn without grace, whereas the style of the tragedies, no less compact and closely woven, falls gracefully from the shoulder and does not cramp the movement.

Movement: there lies the weakness of the early plays: there are no *gestures*, as it were, and little variety of speed. Paradoxes, proverbs and euphuisms litter one's path.

> Smooth runs the water where the brook is deep.
>   (*2 Henry VI*.)

> The smallest worm will turn being trodden on.
>   (*3 Henry VI*.)

> Seems he a dove?   His feathers are but borrowed,
> For he's disposed as is the hateful raven.
> Is he a lamb?   His skin is surely lent him,
> For he's inclined as is the ravenous wolf.
>
> (2 Henry VI.)
>
> Or as the snake rolled in the flowering bank.
>
> (2 Henry VI.)

Even in *Romeo and Juliet* the diction sometimes impedes the pace:

> O serpent heart hid with a flowering face,
> Did ever dragon keep so fair a cave?
> Dove-feathered raven!   Wolfish-ravening lamb!

All the animals in and out of Aesop are herded together with the heroes of Greece and Rome. The similes are careful and lengthy. Here are two from *Henry VI.*, Pt. 3:

> Look, as I blow this feather from my face,
> And as the air blows it to me again,
> Obeying with my wind when I do blow,
> And yielding to another when it blows,
> Commanded always by the greater gust:
> Such is the lightness of you common men.
>
> Why then I do but dream on sovereignty;
> Like one that stands upon a promontory,
> And spies a far-off shore where he would tread,
> Wishing his feet were equal with his eye,
> And chides the sea that sunders him from hence,
> Saying, he'll lade it dry to have his way.

These are straightforward, excellent in their way; but it is the narrative, not the dramatic way, the way of *Sohrab and Rustum*. There is a natural pause at the end of each line and the lines are piled one upon the other. This form of versification which is so common in all his work previous to 1600 is the versification of poetry which is to be read, not spoken. It is the versification of Spenser, of *Venus and Adonis* and *Lucrece*, and it was some time before Shakespeare grew out of it. For one thing, it jingles prettily, for another, it helps to increase the speed. The actor can take the lines at a run. We will take an example from each play.

> The time was once when thou unurged wouldst vow
> That never words were music to thine ear,
> That never object pleasing in thine eye,
> That never touch well welcome to thine hand,
> That never meat sweet-savoured in thy taste,
> Unless I spake or look'd or touch'd or carved to thee.
>
> *(Comedy of Errors.)*

> His words are bonds, his oaths are oracles,
> His love sincere, his thoughts immaculate,
> His tears pure messengers sent from his heart,
> His heart as far from fraud as heaven from earth.
>
> *(Two Gentlemen.)*

> So many hours must I tend my flock;
> So many hours must I take my rest;
> So many hours must I contemplate;
> So many hours must I sport myself;
> So many days my ewes have been with young;
> So many weeks ere the poor fools will ean;
> So many years ere I shall shear the fleece.
>
> *(3 Henry VI.)*

> O, who can hold a fire in his hand
> By thinking on the frosty Caucasus?
> Or cloy the hungry edge of appetite
> By bare imagination of a feast?
> Or wallow naked in December snow
> By thinking on fantastic summer's heat? *(Richard II.)*

Our instruments to melancholy bells,
Our wedding cheer to a sad burial feast,
Our solemn hymns to sullen dirges change,
Our bridal flowers serve for a buried corse,
And all things change them to the contrary.

(*Romeo and Juliet.*)

You, Lord Archbishop,
Whose see is by a civil peace maintained,
Whose beard the silver hand of peace hath touched,
Whose learning and good letters peace hath tutored,
Whose white investments figure innocence. . . .

(*2 Henry IV.*)

If ever you have look'd on better days,
If ever been where bells have knoll'd to church,
If ever sat at any good man's feast,
If ever from your eyelids wip'd a tear
And know what 'tis to pity and be pitied,
Let gentleness my strong enforcement be.

(*As You Like It.*)

This might best be called *stanza movement*. The Shakespearian sonnet (*e.g.* LXVI.) is similar, but on a rather larger scale. Out of numerous examples in *Lucrece*, I quote one:

Let him have time to tear his curled hair,
Let him have time against himself to rave,
Let him have time of Time's help to despair,
Let him have time to live a loathed slave,
Let him have time a beggar's orts to crave ;

(981.)

and one from Spenser:

I hate to speak, my voice is spent with crying,
I hate to hear, loud plaints have dulled my ears,
I hate to taste, for food withholds my dying,
I hate to see, mine eyes are dimmed with tears,

> I hate to smell, no sweet on earth is left,
> I hate to feel, my flesh is numb'd with fears;
> So all my senses from me are bereft.　　(*Daphnaida.*)

The movement is not uncommon in other plays of the time, in Greene and Kyd.　A subtle usage occurs in *Arden of Feversham*.

> Wilt thou not look?　Is all thy love o'erwhelmed?
> Wilt thou not hear?　What malice stops thine ears?
> Why speak'st thou not?　What silence ties thy tongue?
> Thou hast been sighted as the eagle is,
> And heard as quickly as the fearful hare,
> And spoke as smoothly as an orator,
> When I have bid thee hear or see or speak;
> And art thou sensible in none of these?

The accumulation and the management of the pauses are skilful.　The speed rises and then comes to rest. Marlowe's verse climbs the same staircase, but he never jingles, not even in the Zenocrate refrain: there is less repetition.　One foot is always planted firmly upon the next stair—they succeed each other.　Shakespeare in the quotations above seems to draw himself up one foot at a time.

In close combination with this method of laying line upon line, we may take the Shakespearian habit of accumulating words, a rhetorical device which also increases the speed.　It survives in a modified form even in his final style.　In *Venus and Adonis*:

> Were I hard-featured, foul, or wrinkled-old,
> Ill-nurtured, crooked, churlish, harsh in voice,
> O'erworn, despiséd, rheumatic and cold,
> Thick-sighted, barren, lean, and lacking juice,
> Then might'st thou pause . . .

In *Love's Labour's Lost*:

> This wimpled, whining, purblind, wayward boy,
> This senior-junior, giant-dwarf, Dan Cupid;
> Regent of love-rhymes, lord of folded arms,
> The anointed sovereign of sighs and groans,
> Liege of all loiterers and malcontents,
> Dread prince of plackets, king of codpieces,
> Sole imperator and great general
> Of trotting 'paritors.

Regent, lord, sovereign, liege, prince, king, imperator, general: this is the "dictionary method" of Burton. John of Gaunt's England speech, Othello's "Farewell, the pluméd wars", Macbeth's "Innocent sleep . . ." provide other examples among many. The device is worth noticing, as one reads, for two reasons: first, because it tended to break down end-stopping; secondly, because, like scales and five-finger exercises, as it were, it makes the vocabulary richer and more flexible.

This practice is characteristic of Shakespeare's style; it contributed to his development. But it is not the cause of the complete although gradual change between his two styles. The child is father of the man, the first brought forth the second; but there comes a year when the gulf between the two seems a wide one. That year was roughly 1600. It marks a change in Shakespeare and in Elizabethan poetic diction. How did the change in his style come about? What was the reason of it? I have never found that critics answered these questions.

III

DEVELOPMENT AND TRANSITION
TO THE MATURE STYLE

THERE ARE, on my own reading, two reasons:

(1) A reaction against the diction and versification of the day, *which led to the study of prose*.

(2) Character and dramatic realism breaking through fashions and conventions.

The two go hand in hand, for the study of character occasioned, if it did not cause, the reaction.

Language is the subject of *Love's Labour's Lost*. Shakespeare is still half enchanted by the golden net in which he is entangled. Armado, with his fire-new words and congruent epithetons; Boyet, honey-tongued, wit's pedlar; Berowne, conceit's expositor, represent three degrees of the courtly and the fantastical. The play jangles with puns and parodies, showing a nimble, critical, satirical spirit. (I can add little to Pater's *Appreciation*.) A remark of Holofernes deserves attention:

> Ovidius Naso was the man; and why indeed, Naso, but for smelling out the odoriferous flowers of fancy, the jerks of invention? *Imitari* is nothing; so doth the hound his master, the ape his keeper, the 'tired horse his rider.

The odoriferous flowers soon withered. Shakespeare was never as seduced by Ovid as were the university wits.

The play also gives the reaction against verbal fashions and imitations to " russet yeas and kersey noes ".

> *Berowne.* My love to thee is sound sans crack or flaw.
> *Rosalind.* Sans " sans ", I pray you.
> *Berowne.*   Yet I have a trick
> Of the old rage; bear with me, I am sick;
> I'll leave it by degrees.

And Shakespeare did. The dramatic reality of Berowne and the tragic situation tumbles over the card house. " Honest plain words best suit the ear of grief."

There are plenty of other instances of Shakespeare tilting at the diction of the day. Take Demetrius:

> O, Helen, goddess, nymph, perfect, divine;
> To what my love shall I compare thine eyne?
> Crystal is muddy. O, how ripe in show
> Thy lips, those kissing cherries, tempting grow;
> This pure congealed white, high Taurus snow,
> Fann'd with the eastern wind turns to a crow,
> When thou holdst up thine hand.

It is written with the tongue in the cheek, an amusing parody.

Twelfth Night has many little touches; the clown's —" Oh! this age. A sentence is but a cheveril glove to a good wit; how quickly the wrong side may be turned outward ", and " words are grown so false, I am loath to prove reason with them ", and " I might say ' element ', but the word is overworn ", and " Vent my folly! He has heard that word of some great man, and now applies it to a fool. I prithee now ungird thy strangeness and tell me what I shall vent to my lady "; or Sir Andrew's admiration for Viola's " Jerks of invention ". " Odours, pregnant, and vouchsafed.

L

I'll get 'em all three ready." Or take the musicians in *Romeo and Juliet* scratching their heads over " music with her silver sound ", or Speed, " your old vice still; mistake the word ".

Everywhere one remarks this awareness and sensibility to words and with it an increasing feeling of reaction from the artificial and the pretty. Crystal, cherries, the lily and rose, tears of pearl, the buds of youth, and other similar conceits cease, with a few exceptions to be considered elsewhere, in the later plays.

The reaction against rhetoric and bombast is too obvious to be dwelt on. The parody put in the mouth of ancient Pistol takes a more passionate note in Hamlet's denunciation of the players. Every tongue had caught the trick of Marlowe and Kyd. Their blank verse had taken the town by storm, just as *Poems and Ballads* took the undergraduates and set them marching and chanting up and down King's Parade. Shakespeare turned to prose:

> *Orlando.* Good day, and happiness, dear Rosalind.
> *Jaques.* Nay, then, God be wi' you, an you talk in blank verse.
> (*Exit.*)

Character or rather a particular character is interfering. Beside Berowne place Richard III., Hotspur, the Bastard. They all speak with the same accent; they are all realistic, commonsensical, prosaic, energetic figures. They take the verse into their own hands and break down the barriers of diction. Gloucester gives the point of view of them all.

> Because I cannot flatter and speak fair,
> Smile in men's faces, smooth, deceive, and cog,
> Duck with French nods and apish courtesy,
> I must be held a rancorous enemy.
> Cannot a plain man live and think no harm,
> But thus his simple truth must be abused
> By silken, sly, insinuating Jacks?

Or take Faulconbridge's ridicule of the citizen of Angiers—

> Here's a large mouth indeed,
> That spits forth death and mountains, rocks and seas,
> Talks as familiarly of roaring lions
> As maids of thirteen do of puppy-dogs. . . .
> 'Zounds, I was never so bethumped with words
> Since I first called my brother's father dad ;

and of the Dauphin's Petrarchian conceits—

> Drawn in the flattering tablet of her eye!
> Hang'd in the frowning wrinkle of her brow!
> And quarter'd in her heart, he doth espy
> Himself love's traitor: this is pity now,
> That hang'd and drawn and quarter'd, there should be
> In such a love so vile a lout as he.

One regrets that he was not present instead of Hubert to counter Arthur's frigid fancies over the burning coal.

Take Hotspur's account of the lord " perfumed like a milliner "—

> he made me mad
> To see him shine so brisk and smell so sweet
> And talk so like a waiting gentlewoman
> Of guns and drums and wounds ;

or his trouncing of Glendower—

> I had rather be a kitten and cry mew
> Than one of these same metre ballad-mongers;
> I had rather hear a brazen canstick turned,
> Or a dry wheel grate on the axle tree;
> And that would set my teeth nothing on edge,
> Nothing so much as mincing poetry:
> 'Tis like the forc'd gait of a shuffling nag;

or last with Lady Percy—

Not yours, in good sooth. Heart, you swear like a comfit-maker's wife. Not you, " in good sooth ", and " as true as I live ", and " as God shall mend me ", and " as sure as day ".

> And giv'st such sarcenet surety for thy oaths,
> As if thou never walk'dst further than Finsbury.
> Swear me, Kate, like a lady as thou art,
> A good mouth-filling oath; and leave " in sooth ",
> And such protest of pepper gingerbread,
> To velvet-guards and Sunday-citizens.

All these passages have critical significance. I do not fall into the snare of identifying Shakespeare with his *dramatis personae* and making his views theirs; but these voices demanded a new medium, verse which will allow colloquial emphases and prose order, or else prose itself, the prose which Hamlet and Edmund and Iago were to speak. Dramatic effect must war with poetic decoration. In the early plays it is the characters who are really alive that mould and modify the verse. Thus the nurse in *Romeo and Juliet* in the famous speech (Act I. Sc. 3) with its repetitions, parentheses and oratio recta, breaks up the rhythms:

> I never should forget it; " Wilt thou not, Jule," quoth he;

and her—

> And a good lady, and a wise, and virtuous,

and Capulet's rebukes of Tybalt. In the *Midsummer Night's Dream* the vitality of the dialogue begins to get the better not only of metre but even of rhyme. Repetition again is a useful instrument of realism.

> She, sweet lady, dotes,
> Devoutly dotes, dotes to idolatry,
> Upon this spotted and inconstant man.

> Am I not Hermia? Are not you Lysander?

> Is't not enough, is't not enough, young man,
> That I did never, no, nor never can,
> Deserve a sweet look from Demetrius' eye,
> But you must flout my insufficiency?
> Good troth you do me wrong, good sooth you do,
> In such disdainful manner me to woo.

The transitional period begins with *The Merchant of Venice* (1596) The clowns, old Gobbo and Launcelot speak prose; that is nothing new Portia and Nerissa have a light prose scene, where Julia and Lucetta had been hampered by verse. It is, however, antithetical, euphuistic prose: "The brain may devise laws for the blood, but a hot temper leaps o'er a cold decree; such a hare is madness the youth, to skip o'er the meshes of good counsel the cripple". This is of the same order as Hotspur's "I tell you, my lord fool, out of this nettle, danger, we pluck the flower, safety". Sebastian in *Twelfth Night* is another who "speaks holiday"—"My determinate voyage is mere extravagancy". The style is excellently parodied by Falstaff. But the significant fact is that Shylock speaks prose, and he is of tragic dimensions. He speaks prose, not all the way through, certainly, but at his best moment (Act III. 1). It is mannered prose, as Shakespearian prose always is, antithetical, accumulative in effect, like the verse passages already noted: but it is passionate. Above all, for the moment character has banished verse, drama has banished poetry.

What follows? *Henry IV.*, *Henry V.*, *Much Ado*, *As You Like It*. Every one is speaking prose, court prose or comic prose, and Shakespeare is mocking blank verse or transposing the chronicles. The characters are taking the words into their own hands. Falstaff, Quickly, Shallow, Caius, Mine Host, Beatrice and Benedict, Fluellen, Rosalind, all are alive and speaking prose, both light and serious, while Hotspur rattles his metrical fetters.

In *The Merchant of Venice* also Shakespeare rides his verse with ease over flat country. That is to say he runs on in a natural colloquial way; for instance, Portia's speech, " It is enacted in the laws of Venice " (Act IV. 1). Inversion is comparatively rare, ornament has been pruned away, and for a short period Shakespeare's verse is less mannered than his prose. Jaques is colloquial in verse.

The new style was beginning, packed with matter, a style that could gallop at a touch, with freer rhythms and higher emotional pressure. We shall find the first hint of it in the second part of *Henry IV.*

> O God, that one might read the book of fate,
> And see the revolution of the times
> Make mountains level, and the continent—
> Weary of solid firmness—melt itself
> Into the sea!   And, other times, to see
> The beachy girdle of the ocean
> Too wide for Neptune's hips; how chances mock,
> And changes fill the cup of alteration
> With divers liquors!   O, if this were seen,
> The happiest youth, viewing his progress through,
> What perils past, what crosses to ensue,
> Would shut the book and sit him down and die.
> 'Tis not ten years gone
> Since Richard and Northumberland, great friends . . .

That is the accent of Hamlet. We have the pauses and parentheses and exclamations, the changes of construction, the broken and shortened lines of the tragedies. *The study of dramatic prose made Shakespeare master of dramatic verse.*

After King Henry's speech above, comes Warwick's—

> There is a history in all men's lives
> Figuring the nature of the times deceased . . .

which is a pair to Brutus's—

> There is a tide in the affairs of men
> Which taken at the flood leads on to fortune.

This one might call the Greek Chorus manner. The many examples of it in the chronicle plays gave place to the soliloquies of the tragedies. It is weighty and controlled, something between the poetic and the dramatic, tending very often towards the rhetorical.

Pater speaking of the opening lines of *Love's Labour's Lost* notes the " monumental " manner of the *Sonnets*, and it is in passages in this manner that the earlier Shakespeare excels. Time is not rarely the subject, and the model, Ovid,

> Jamque opus exegi, quod nec Jovis ira, nec ignis,
> Nec poterit ferrum, nec edax abolere vetustas.

and the " Exegi monumentum " of Horace. *Lucrece* has fine stanzas and there are similar lines in the *Sonnets*.

> Time's thievish progress to eternity. (*Sonnets.*)

> Thou ceaseless lackey to eternity. (*Lucrece.*)

> Let fame that all hunt after in their lives
> Live registered upon our brazen tombs,
> And then grace us in the disgrace of death;
> When spite of cormorant devouring Time,
> The endeavour of this present breath may buy
> The honour which shall bate his scythe's keen edge,
> And make us heirs of all eternity. (*Love's Labour's Lost.*)

> When I have seen by Time's fell hand defaced
> The rich proud cost of outworn buried age;
> When sometimes lofty towers I see down-raz'd
> And brass eternal slave to mortal rage. (*Sonnets.*)

> To ruinate proud buildings with thine hours
> And smear with dust their glittering golden towers.
> (*Lucrece.*)

When Shakespeare approaches the sublime before 1600, it is in this serious, classical, monumental way. But although eminently suitable for reflection, it is not fast or flexible enough for soliloquy. Even when raised to its highest emotional power, it is not dramatic.

Lucrece, Constance, Faulconbridge, Berowne *rail* on death and time and women and commodity. But if they move us, it is by rhetoric. In the soliloquies of Hamlet and Othello and Macbeth lies the conflict of passion and reason. They do not rail.

This style is the first which Shakespeare perfected. It is as weighty as Jonson but more golden. It survives in its final and most successful form in *Julius Caesar*, in *Measure for Measure*, in the great speech of Ulysses in *Troilus and Cressida*.

IV

THE MATURE STYLE

CRITICS HAVE TENDED to classify the plays written after 1600 according either to their spiritual character and atmosphere or their versification. Statistics of feminine endings and rhymed couplets, divisions into "the tragic period", "the comedies of reconciliation", "on the heights" and "in the depths" are not irrelevant for the consideration of Shakespeare's style, yet preoccupation with these questions leaves more fundamental characteristics unemphasised if not unexplored. By 1600 Shakespeare had learnt all there was to learn from Marlowe and Kyd, Peele and Lyly; he had wearied of the stiff and pompous gait of the padded end-stopped verse of the day. Even in his earliest work he seldom minces, swaggers or shuffles as they often do. He learnt how to walk in verse, how to use the decasyllabic line with economy and simplicity and freedom. *In a word, he reduced blank verse to the level of prose.* No other dramatist before the end of the century achieved this, although it came naturally enough to Shakespeare's successors, notably to Massinger. And this achievement was absolutely essential for two reasons. First, because Shakespeare wrote drama and not only poetry, and therefore the blank verse measure had to be made adaptable to every purpose and capable of the functions of prose. Secondly, because, until he had reduced blank verse to the level of prose, he could not create and develop a style of his own. He had to start

" from par ", as it were, instead of being content to modify, inlay or build upon the style of his predecessors. As we have seen, he undermined their methods by rhetorical *tirades*, put into the mouths of his more realistic characters, of Berowne and Faulconbridge and Hotspur, and then discarded verse in favour of prose. Mercutio and Shylock are the forerunners; Falstaff, Tearsheet, Shallow, Quickly and Jaques follow. Had *The Tempest* been written in this period, Caliban, we may surmise, would have spoken prose. For some years Shakespeare occupied himself with practising and perfecting the art. Although at first he employed it mainly for comedy scenes, both court comedy and low comedy, he began to experiment further. Just as he had naturalised blank verse, inducing it to undertake such unattractive duties as, for instance, the exposition of the Salic law, without clumsiness, so, *vice versa*, he sought to raise prose to a higher level, a level not far below some of the best verse passages in his earlier dramas. Worthy of note in this respect is the scene between Henry V. and Michael Williams, which contains such passages as these:

King Henry. For though I speak it to you, I think the king is but a man as I am: the violet smells to him as it doth to me; the element shows to him as it doth to me; all his senses have but human conditions; his ceremonies laid by, in his nakedness he appears but a man; and though his affections are higher mounted than ours, when they stoop, they stoop with the like wing;

and—

Besides, there is no king, be his cause never so spotless, if it come to the arbitrement of swords, can try it out with all unspotted soldiers.

Some, peradventure, have on them the guilt of premeditated and contrived murder; some of beguiling virgins with the broken seals of perjury; some, making the wars their bulwark, that have before gored the gentle bosom of peace with pillage and robbery. Now, if these men have defeated the law and outrun native punishment, though they can outstrip men, they have no wings to fly from God; war is his beadle, war is his vengeance; so that here men are punished for before-breach of the king's laws in now the king's quarrel; where they feared the death they have borne life away, and where they would be safe they perish.

This is well reasoned and composed, more simple and serious than Shakespeare's usual prose style. In the historical plays the nobles, as a rule, speak verse, the commoners and comic characters prose. The incident in this scene, in which his majesty " appears but as a common man ", demands, of course, that he should speak prose, but this does not affect my argument that the style deserves notice. Let us examine the subsequent plays and pursue the study of Shakespeare's prose style.

It is important that in *Julius Caesar* the oration of Brutus is a mannered piece of prose, while Antony's simple, if more emotional, appeal is in verse. Prose also is used for Casca's scornful description of the crown being offered to Cæsar. This is in character; for he is a blunt fellow, whose " rudeness is a sauce to his good wit ". That is to say, he belongs to the same family as the Bastard and Hotspur whose dissatisfaction with the medium of verse has already been commented on. In this scene (I. 2) Casca is allowed the natural freedom to which they aspired.

In the three comedies, which belong to the same period as *Julius Caesar*, prose predominates over verse.

In *Much Ado*, the earliest of the three, there is a simple division; the verse portions all centre round Hero, the tragic character. So also in *Twelfth Night* the love-sick Orsino speaks verse and Viola, being his page, has in his company to follow his example. But whenever she escapes from the infectious sentimental atmosphere of his court, she tends to slip into the natural speech of her sisters, Beatrice and Rosalind; in her first embassy to Olivia, for instance. Olivia and Viola have to be equally at home in prose and verse, as they are the links with the comic characters. The distribution of prose and verse in *As You Like It* is more curious. The first scene is a long and clumsy piece of exposition in prose, much inferior to the similar scene in *Much Ado*, and the opening of *Romeo and Juliet*. The pro-logues which introduce *Henry V.* and *Troilus and Cressida* rivet the attention; the immediate plunge *in medias res* in *Hamlet*, *Othello*, *Antony and Cleopatra* and *The Tempest* is infinitely more dramatic.

Verse is spoken in the forest of Arden, prose by Rosalind, Celia and Touchstone, who belong to the workaday world. Even Jaques who affects to scorn it, makes his best speeches in poetry, and contrary to the usual custom, shepherds and shepherdesses speak verse, where the hero and heroine, the son and daughter of dukes, speak prose.

To make a rough generalisation about these plays, which are perfect of their kind and the consummation of Shakespeare's earlier period, we may say that verse is reserved for those characters who have no sense of humour, and prose for those who are most alive.

By the beginning of the century, then, Shakespeare
had mastered a new medium, and in the tragedies he
reaped the reward of several years' experience. Practice
in prose taught him to create a new kind of verse,
richer and more natural, swifter and more varied.
Troilus and Cressida and *Hamlet*, which mark the transition to the new style, have a great deal in common.
No other play seems so packed with matter, or to
touch life at so many points, as do these two.   Even
Antony and Cleopatra is no exception.   The matter
there is more digested; there is more economy, more
ease. *Troilus* has not the unity of *Hamlet*, but the
same prodigality marks them both and sets them apart
from all Shakespeare's other work.   Most essential
to both, and the expression of that prodigality, is the
prose element.   It is significant that Cressida speaks
prose, as readily as Rosalind, Beatrice and Viola, and
when she falters into verse, utters weak couplets however tragic the occasion (I. 2. 306; V. 2. 104).   Poetry
is Troilus's natural speech, except in one scene where
she flirts with him (III. 2), and as a rule she lets him
do most of the talking (IV. 4).

What would these two plays be without their prose
scenes and characters?   In the one, Pandarus, Thersites, Ajax; the long and excellent comedy scene when
the Trojan heroes pass over the stage, the thumb-nail
sketch of Helen and Paris.   In the other, all Hamlet's
best scenes with his contemporaries Rosencrantz and
Guildenstern, with Ophelia, with Osric, with the
Players, with the Gravediggers.   These show him in
his intercourse with the world, as others saw him; the

soliloquies as he saw himself. And it is the complete naturalness of the prose scenes which makes the soliloquies so convincing. The one is the complement of the other.

In *Troilus and Cressida* the prose mostly consists of the execrations of that indecent chorus Thersites, who is a great improvement on Parolles, and the rival of Falstaff in vocabulary, if not in intellect. What a relief his oaths and filth are after the lisp and compliment of Euphues. Yet Thersites has *style*. "What art thou Greek?" cries Hector. "Art thou of blood and honour?" "No, no, I am a rascal; a scurvy railing knave; a very filthy rogue." And when surprised by Margarelon; "I am a bastard too; I love bastards; I am a bastard begot, bastard instructed, bastard in mind, bastard in valour, in everything illegitimate; . . . . if the son of whore fight for a whore, he tempts judgement. Farewell, bastard."

It is not perhaps necessary to emphasise the quality of the prose in *Hamlet*. Here are passages which represent the highest point Shakespeare ever reached in this medium; the famous outburst, "What a piece of work is man", the meditations over Yorick's skull, the parable of the recorder, the renunciation of Ophelia. And, I repeat, it is the excellence and the importance of the prose which separates *Hamlet* from, and in many ways sets it above, all the other plays. Shakespeare's first sublime character, Falstaff, was created in prose; Hamlet, his greatest, in both elements; Cleopatra, the third, in poetry. There is a large proportion of prose in *Measure for Measure*,

the play which is thought to be next to *Hamlet*, chrono-
logically; not only the many low characters but also
the Duke himself has many prose scenes, in which
the burden of exposition lies heavily upon him. His
prose is neither individual nor profound. Altogether
Measure for Measure strikes one as a play " in the
rough ", only half-fashioned and then abandoned,
denied the infinite pains and continual revision which
went to its predecessor.

In *Othello* and *Lear* we have the prose villain.
Iago is of common clay and his mind is as dirty as
Lucio's or Pandar's. The difference between him
and his master is heightened by the different medium.
And he is intellectual, like Falstaff and Hamlet; that
is better marked by prose; Othello is emotional.
Iago's verse soliloquies are pedestrian. He touches
a higher note in Othello's company, *because then he
affects honesty*. The cynical prose which is natural
to him would be out of place there. Blank verse is
part of his rôle, so to speak.

Edmund presents a slight contrast. He is more
noble both in blood and temper than the Moorship's
Ancient. At the beginning of the play, in the scene
with Gloucester and Edgar (I. 2), it might be Iago
speaking; particularly the speech—" This is the
excellent foppery of the world, that when we are sick
in fortune—often the surfeit of our own behaviour—
we make guilty of our disasters the sun, the moon, and
the stars ". Compare Iago's " Virtue! a fig! 'Tis
in ourselves that we are thus or thus." But at the
end he deserves to rank rather beside Macbeth, and

higher, for he says: " Some good I mean to do, despite of mine own nature ". Throughout the last act he speaks fine verse.

In *Othello* the prose is as free as in *Hamlet*; in *Lear* it is more mannered. Take, for example, Gloucester's: " Love cools, friendship falls off, brothers divide; in cities mutinies; in countries discord; in palaces treason; and the bond cracked between son and father ". Or Edgar's speech (III. 4. 84), and Lear's answer: " Why, thou wert better in thy grave than to answer with thy uncovered body this extremity of the skies. Is man no more than this? Consider him well. Thou owest the worm no silk, the beast no hide, the sheep no wool, the cat no perfume. Ha, here's three on's are sophisticated; thou art the thing itself; unaccommodated man is no more but such a poor bare forked animal as thou art. Off, off, you lendings. Come, unbutton here."

After *Hamlet*, Shakespeare's prose is never again so subtle. After *Lear* he never again employs the prose medium to such good purpose. Why is this? Because of his immense progress in blank verse. He had fashioned himself a unique instrument and he knew all the niceties of its conduct. The blank verse of the tragic period reached its highest point in *Antony and Cleopatra*. In the final comedies it was carried to an almost fantastic extreme. The rhythms became more and more resolved, asyndeton and anacoluthon more frequent, until the metre and syntax were traditionally no longer those of prose or verse, but both seemed fused together and interchangeable.

M

There are scenes in *Antony and Cleopatra* which, in
their dramatic significance, correspond to parts of
Hamlet.   But Cleopatra, unlike Hamlet, whom as a
dramatic creation she in other ways much resembles
(except that she has a partner with whom to share the
stage and divide the attention of the audience), does
not speak prose.   One is hardly conscious of this, her
dialogue is so natural.   Her second scene with the
messenger (III. 3), if it had been composed in 1602,
would probably have been a prose scene; none the
less she is not at all hampered by the metre, which is
much broken up among the protagonists.   It is true
that there is the same ingenious conversion of blank
verse into dialogue in the scenes that take place on the
ramparts at Elsinore; they are not in prose because,
for one thing, they are not a character scene; for
another, the atmosphere demands verse.

The main functions of the prose in the later drama
of Shakespeare are as follows: First, in those cases
where a character is mad or affects madness, or is
suffering from hysteria and is, as it were, beyond control.
Examples of this are the distractions of Ophelia, the
sleep-walking of Lady Macbeth, the mock lunacy of
Edgar.   Again, in *Othello*, Act IV. 1, Iago works up
the Moor to such a pitch that he bursts into prose and
falls into a trance.   Later on in the same scene, when
almost out of his mind with agony and hate, he speaks
prose.

I would have him nine years a-killing. A fine woman! A fair
woman! A sweet woman! . . . My heart is turned to stone. I strike
it and it hurts my hand. O, the world hath not a sweeter creature; she

might lie by an emperor's side and command him tasks. . . . So
delicate with her needle! An admirable musician! . . . Of so high
and plenteous wit and invention! . . . but yet the pity of it, Iago. . . .
I will chop her into messes.

Although this is as telling as any of Hamlet's prose,
yet prose it is. Iago has reduced Othello to his own
element, but assumes once more the dignity of blank
verse on the entry of Lodovico, the envoy from Venice.

As further evidence on this point may be cited
King Lear, Act IV. 6. 81-192. Edgar comments:

> O, matter and impertinency mixed!
> Reason in madness!

And, roughly speaking, the matter of the King's
speeches is in verse (110-130, 165-177, 181-186), the
impertinency in prose.

On several occasions prose is used for a realistic
scene; for instance, the soothsayer scene in the first
act of *Antony and Cleopatra*, which gives all the atmosphere of the Alexandrian court. Also the serving-men
at the beginning and end of *Coriolanus*, IV. 5. In the
same play the Roman ladies have a quiet and natural
prose scene, in which they sit at home and sew; a
contrast to the tremendous poetic appeal made by
Volumnia in the last act. Elsewhere prose is employed
where the tension is relaxed, to give the audience
breath; thus an otherwise unimportant scene between
a Roman and a Volsce follows on Volumnia's and
Virgilia's cursing of the tribunes.

In those intriguing and unsatisfactory pieces,
Cymbeline and *The Winter's Tale*, prose is heavily,

casually employed, as a beast of burden. Posthumus
and Iachimo strike their fatal bargain in a long prose
scene. Camillo and Archidamus idly introduce *The
Winter's Tale*, while, in addition to Autolycus and the
Shepherd and the Clown, we have three prosy gentlemen who dish up the story again in the last act. *The
Tempest* is superior to these two plays in this as in other
respects.

Without pushing one's conclusions too far, it is
time to attempt a summary. The first and obvious
use of prose in Elizabethan drama is for low and comic
characters, for servants and clowns, such as Speed
and Gobbo. Shakespeare achieved his first successes
in character in this realistic medium, Shallow and
Quickly and Fluellen, to name only three. Gradually
the more important characters caught the infec-
tion. Faulconbridge, Gloucester, Berowne, Hotspur
clamoured for prose, Mercutio, the first tragic character, Shylock and Casca won it. If *Coriolanus* had
been written at the time of *King John*, Menenius, like
the Bastard, would have spoken verse. Further, when
Shakespeare, hampered by the limitations of the blank
verse of Marlowe and Kyd, turned to the court
comedy of Lyly, he created in prose Rosalind and
Beatrice. In these he made court comedy more
realistic, in Falstaff he raised low comedy to a different
level. Falstaff is an intellectual character. In him,
in Hamlet, in Iago, in Edmund, and (in lesser degrees)
in Thersites and Menenius, Shakespeare used prose
for a more philosophical purpose, for reasoning, while

verse suits more emotional expression.   Shakespeare
with more invention and subtlety used prose to suggest
certain *traits* of character, worldliness perhaps, or
cynicism, or sense of humour (like Enobarbus), or
for persons of commoner clay, not necessarily by birth,
but by disposition; Sebastian, for instance, in *The
Tempest*, brother to the King of Naples.   And in
Act I. Sc. 2 it is to be noted that Stephano and
Trinculo speak prose, while the monster, Caliban,
speaks verse.   Similarly in *Othello*, Act IV. 3, the
matter-of-fact Emilia, except for her last speech,
intersperses Desdemona's verse with prose.

*Above all, Shakespeare found himself dramatically
in prose*, and his apprenticeship in that element helped
him during those middle years in which he threw over
his old models and created a new form of blank verse.
It is true that as he advanced and elaborated that new
style he was able more and more to dispense with
prose.   But the greatness of *Othello* and *Troilus and
Cressida* and *King Lear*, and more particularly of
Hamlet, arises from the combination of both which
enabled him to create his characters, as it were, in
another dimension.   Although prose is not entirely
eliminated from *Antony and Cleopatra*, it is a *tour de
force* in the use of verse.   After that, Shakespeare let
his obligations as a dramatist slide; he exploited his
verse style recklessly, and, where he did not feel
inspired to write poetry, filled in the gaps with prose.

V

A POINT IN VERSIFICATION

ANY IRREGULARITY which contributes to the breaking down of the stiff verse of the early drama deserves attention. Marlowe's turbulent flood surmounted the end-stopping of Sackville and Dorset, and replaced the couplet movement with paragraph movement. But more important, because essentially dramatic, is the practice of leaving the decasyllable unfinished, of using a half line, not only for exclamation and parenthesis, but also to mark a strong pause. We will follow out Shakespeare's method on this point.

In *Romeo and Juliet* we have a few, a very few examples. Most of the soliloquies, including Romeo's death speech, run straight through to the end. We have, however, the effective—

> It is my lady; O, it is my love:
> O, that she knew she were;

and at a dramatic moment, Juliet's—

> Nurse!   What should she do here?
> My dismal scene I needs must act alone.
> Come, vial.

The one or two other instances (one in the nurse's realistic speech) are less interesting. In *The Merchant of Venice* we have equally few, the best being Shylock's " Say this " (I. 3. 126), Arragon's " Lastly " (II. 9. 14), and Portia's—

> I would be trebled twenty times myself;
> A thousand times more fair, ten thousand times
> More rich;
> That only to stand high in your account . . .

an overflowing which is absolutely natural and charming.

In *Henry IV.*, Pts. 1 and 2, it is still rare.   Hotspur, be it noted, has several of them, *Nay, 'sblood*, and other interjections.   In *Julius Caesar* we do not find it in the big speeches.   Brutus says in a short soliloquy, " I have not slept ", and it seems weighty in its isolation. Cassius in the middle of a speech ends a paragraph effectively with a short line, but has another of the same length, only two lines later, which is weakening and holds up the speaker (I. 3. 71-73).

But with *Troilus and Cressida* and *Hamlet*, in this detail as in so many other matters, there is a tremendous change.   Twice we have a short line in the very prologue to *Troilus*, that studied piece of grandiloquence.   The middle paragraph begins in fine style—

> To Tenedos they come,

and closes

> Sperr up the sons of Troy.

Then in the first great council scene we have seven or more examples.   Agamemnon opens with the word " Princes ".   The tremendous oration of Ulysses (I. 3. 75-138), with its extraordinary mastery of speed, begins thus:

> Troy, yet upon his basis, had been down,
> And the great Hector's sword had lacked a master,
> But for these instances.
> The specialty of rule hath been neglected.

How important the half line is here, how dramatic!
The pause throws the emphasis on to the following
line which is the text of the speech.   Ulysses employs
the break on other occasions; with mock impressive-
ness—

> As amply titled as Achilles is,
> By going to Achilles;

and with studied effect—

> . . . I was much rapt in this;
> And apprehended here immediately
> The unknown Ajax.
> Heavens, what a man is there, a very horse . . .

and ten lines farther down, rubbing in the same lesson
into Achilles—

> . . . Ajax renowned.   O heavens, what some men do,
> While some men leave to do.

In his next speech Ulysses breaks the metre three
times; once after the fifth, once after the fourth, and
once after the seventh syllable, thereby gaining in
freedom, naturalness and variety.

In *Hamlet* the short line is common at the beginning
and end and in the middle of speeches.   Thus when
Horatio first encounters the ghost, we have " Speak to
me" (twice) and "O, speak!" isolated; and in Hamlet's
scene with the ghost we have four cases—three times
to close a paragraph in the ghost's speech and once for
an interjection, " O most pernicious woman ", in
Hamlet's soliloquy.   In Hamlet's most emotional
outburst—

> O, what a rogue and peasant slave am I,

we have, "For Hecuba", "Yet I", "Ha!" "O!
Vengeance", "A scullion"—five in fifty lines. There
are many other instances, in his scene with Gertrude,
his apology to Laertes, apart from those on the lips of
Polonius and the King.

The last line of the play is

> Go, bid the soldiers shoot.

How much stronger this is than the couplet with which
all the other tragedies close, except *Timon of Athens*,

> Let our drums strike,

and "Assist" in *Coriolanus*. The fact that Shakespeare employed the more masculine and military
ending in these three plays should dispel the romantic
and fanciful interpretation of Hamlet's character
favoured in some quarters. In the remaining plays we
come upon the usage often enough, now for ease and
freedom, now for an exclamation, now to give emphasis
or mark a paragraph. *Measure for Measure* is rich in
instances; Othello's death speech ends—

> I took by the throat the circumcised dog
> And smote him thus! (*Stabs himself*),

and one regrets the later couplet which detracts from
that dramatic gesture. Lear, hovering between prose
and verse, between madness and sanity, has eight out
of twenty broken lines.

This point in versification may seem a trifle, but it
is significant, a straw that shows the direction of the
wind. It is one of the symptoms of the change of

style.   We may trace back to it the new movement in
Elizabethan blank verse.   At first the blank verse was
broken for purposes of dialogue, the first line of B
completing the last line of A's speech.   Then an
incomplete line is used to close a speech (and later a
paragraph), even if the next speaker begins with a
whole decasyllable.   This went hand in hand with
the tendency to shift the pause from the end of the line
or couplet, and resulted in a strong stop in the middle
of the line.   Thus:

> Our revels now are ended.   These our actors,
> As I foretold you, were all spirits and
> Are melted into air, into thin air;
> And, like the baseless fabric of this vision,
> The cloud-capped towers, the gorgeous palaces,
> The solemn temples, the great globe itself,
> Yea, all which it inherit, shall dissolve
> And, like this insubstantial pageant faded,
> Leave not a rack behind.
> 　　　　　　　　　　　We are such stuff
> As dreams are made on, and our little life
> Is rounded with a sleep.

Marlowe's crescendos ended differently, leading up to
a refrain, a full telling line.   This is more subtle, sometimes resting on a high note, sometimes with a dying
fall.   But in the hands of Fletcher and Shirley the
new movement soon lost its subtlety and became a
commonplace.

VI

OBSERVATIONS ON THE DICTION
OF THE LATER PLAYS

IT IS A PROOF of Shakespeare's development that from *Julius Caesar* to *Antony and Cleopatra* the plays demand more individual attention. There is something unique about each of the tragedies, in which the characterisation has the upper hand of the writing and controls the vocabulary to some extent, whereas in *Romeo and Juliet* and the earlier comedies and the verse portions of the histories, the style commands the characters. And in the last period of all, the characters and the plot are sacrificed to the reckless power of expression; in short, to the poetry.

The first symptom of the transition to the new style is, as has been said, to be found in the third act of *King Henry IV.*, Pt. 2, in the soliloquy—

> O God! that one might read the book of fate . . .

And in Warwick's comment following thereon, which is so much in the manner of *Julius Caesar*, we note the phrase—

> Such things become the hatch and brood of time,

which links it with *Hamlet*—

> I do not doubt the hatch and the disclose
> Will be some danger,

and *Measure for Measure*—

> And so in progress to be hatched and born.

In *Henry V.* we begin to have glimpses of a richer, a more rhetorical style. This is most apparent in the prologues, which, although they have less pomp and circumstance than the prologue to *Troilus and Cressida*, are not less powerful, or, to use a favourite word of Shakespeare's in the histories, " puissant ", and are in the same manner. For example, " Assume the port of Mars ", " his brave fleet, with silken streamers the young Phoebus fanning ", " With fatal mouths gaping on girded Harfleur ", and the whole of the prologue to Act IV. They are as polished and studied as any writing of Shakespeare's up to that date.

Now for the first time Latinisms begin to show their heads. Before, they have often been the occasion for satirical comment and fooling. In *Love's Labour's Lost* we have, " Now will I look to this remuneration. Remuneration. O, that's the Latin word for three farthings—remuneration. . . . Why it is a fairer name than French crown . . .": and in 2 *Henry IV.*, Bardolph, in all ignorance, sports " accommodated " to Shallow's great delight: " It comes of *accommodo*; very good; a good phrase ". In *Henry V.* we mark " addiction ", " sequestration " " crescive ", " convocation ", " appro-bation " (which, though it seems common enough, does not occur before this, but is frequent after), " defunction ", " imperfections ", " appertinents " (another word humorously accented in *Love's Labour's Lost*), " sinister " (*Twelfth Night*, 1600; *All's Well*, 1602; *Troilus*, 1602; *Measure for Measure*, 1603–1604; and comically in *Midsummer Night's Dream*, V. 1. 164), " demonstrate ", " demonstrative ", " celerity ",

" attest " (twice; and twice in *Troilus*, once in *Twelfth Night*), " defunct ", " speculation " (*Troilus and Cressida*, *Macbeth*, *Lear*), " perdurable " (*Othello*, *Measure for Measure*), " interim ", " perdition ", " deracinate ", " defective " (*All's Well*, *Coriolanus*, *Hamlet*), " cursorary ", " paction ".

Most of these words belong to the vocabulary of Shakespeare's later style and make their first appearance in *Henry V*. Some are only found between 1599 and 1604. To follow one out more closely, we will take " perdition ". Fluellen says: " The perdition of th'athversary hath been very great, reasonable great ", but then, like other comic characters in Shakespeare, Armado being the extreme case, he rather affects elaborate speech. And it is Sir Toby who next wields it: " This shall end without the perdition of souls ". Then Hamlet, aping court dialect, replies to Osric, " Sir, his definement suffers no perdition in you ". By this time the word is naturalised, and in *Troilus and Cressida* we have—

> Bifold authority, where reason can revolt
> Without perdition.

Then in *Othello* it is a favourite:

> . . . upon certain tidings now arrived, importing the mere perdition of the Turkish fleet, . . .

and, most successfully—

> Perdition catch my soul
> But I do love thee,

and only a scene later—

> To lose't or give't away were such perdition
> As nothing else could match.

In *The Winter's Tale*—

> Commend them and condemn them to her service
> Or to their own perdition,

and twice in *The Tempest*—

> Not so much perdition as an hair
> Betid to any.

> Lingering perdition, worse than any death
> Can be at once.

This is a typical example of the evolution and enriching of Shakespeare's vocabulary. Sometimes a Latinism occurs once or twice before *Henry V.*, but twelve times or even more afterwards. *Love's Labour's Lost*, although it mocks the ornate style and Latin formations, has a few examples in the serious speeches, simply because the words were running in Shakespeare's head. We shall follow out this point further in the other plays, but let us now turn to *Julius Caesar*, which is the prelude to the tragedies and contemporaneous with *Henry V.*, the last of the histories.

It is the first play to have an individual style. At least (if some one should object—" What about *Romeo and Juliet?* "), we may say that it is the first with an individual *dramatic* style. *Romeo and Juliet* is in style the most harmonious and uniform of the earlier plays, and in that respect stands rather apart from the others, but it is a poetic style, the style of the sonnets, and although more ardent, more rich, more rose-coloured, the style of Spenser and the Elizabethan singers.

The style of *Julius Caesar* is clear, grave and bare, Roman, in short; and there is no doubt that Shakespeare was affected by his subject and his material. Perhaps the only other play with the same straight-forward clarity is *The Merchant of Venice*. One distinguishes it mainly from the historical plays in that humanity or characterisation strikes through. Casca is not an advance on Hotspur and Faulconbridge, although, as we have seen, he is more at ease in a prose medium. But Brutus and Cassius are something new. They are conscious of each other's characters; both are introspective and prepare the way for Hamlet and for Macbeth. In consequence the writing of the play is more thoughtful, in a sense, although the diction and versification of the second style has not yet begun to make itself felt. We have, however, one or two symptoms; for instance, *cogitations*, *conceptions*, *retentive*, *posture* (elsewhere only in final plays), *limitation*, *insuppressive*, *emulation*, *prevention*, *interim*, *phantasma*, *contaminate*, *illuminate*, *insupportable*; and

> Have you not made a universal shout,
> That Tiber trembled underneath her banks,
> To hear the replication of your sounds
> Made in her concave shores?

which is, however, at once followed by the familiar early movement—

> And do you now put on your best attire?
> And do you now cull out a holiday?
> And do you now strew flowers in his way
> That comes in triumph over Pompey's blood?

More interesting is the use of metaphors. They are not nearly so thick on the ground as in *Hamlet* and

Troilus and Cressida, but the *evolution* is that of the
later plays.   Here is a good example:

> But if these,
> As I am sure they do, bear *fire* enough
> To *kindle* cowards and to *steel* with valour
> The *melting* spirits of women, then, countrymen,
> What need we any *spur* but our own cause
> To *prick* us to redress?

A little later we have—

> His silver hairs
> Will purchase us a good opinion
> And buy men's voices to commend our deeds,

and both passages anticipate *Macbeth* (I. 7. 24, 32).
Or again—

> . . . such rebel blood
> That will be *thaw'd* from the true quality
> With that which *melteth* fools; I mean *sweet* words,
> Low-crooked curtsies, and base *spaniel fawning*.
> Thy brother by decree is banished;
> If thou dost bend and pray and fawn for him,
> I spurn thee *like a cur* out of my way.

We find the same train of thought in a famous passage
in *Antony and Cleopatra*—

> The hearts
> That *spaniel'd* me at heels, to whom I gave
> Their wishes, do *discandy*, *melt* their *sweets*,
> On blossoming Caesar; and this pine is bark'd
> That overtopp'd them all.

Mr. E. E. Kellett, in his essay on *A Feature of Shakespeare's Style*, cites this passage to show how the puns
and play upon words, so common in Shakespeare, give
us the clue to the combinations of metaphors in the

tragedies; he finds many convincing instances in *Macbeth*, and suggests an explanation of the vexed point in *Othello*, " does tire the ingener "; where, he believes, there is an instantaneous transition of thought from the sense of " to weary " to that of " to adorn ". Of Antony's speech, above, he writes—" Who can keep up with the rapidity of Shakespeare's light fantastic turns of thought? We can see how *discandy* combines both conceptions, that of *sweet* and that of *melting*; we can discern how *spaniel'd* suggested *bark'd*, and how that led to *pine* and *blossoming*, but the speed of transition is beyond us and the intermediate stages are often for ever lost."

I am not satisfied with this explanation. The second part of the metaphor is easy enough and familiar. For we have had in *Lucrece*—

> Ay me! the bark peel'd from the lofty pine,
> His leaves will wither and his sap decay;
> So must my soul, her bark being peel'd away,

and in 2 *Henry VI.*—

> Thus droops this lofty pine and hangs his sprays,

and in *Measure for Measure*—

> You consenting to it
> Would bark the honour from the trunk you bear.

The similes of the early style become condensed and submerged into the metaphors of the mature and final style.

But to return to Mr. Kellett; he ignores the most violent transition, that is from *discandy* to *spaniel'd*.

N

What is the process of thought here? We have exactly the same association in our passage from *Julius Caesar*, *melting*, *sweet*, *spaniel fawning*. (*Spaniel* and *fawning* together are natural enough; compare—

> Spaniel-like the more she spurns my love
> The more it grows and fawneth on her still.
>
> > (*Two Gentlemen.*)

But why *sweet* and *spaniel*, and why *discandy* and *spaniel*? Nor is that all. We have in *Henry IV*., Pt. I.:

> Why what a *candy* deal of courtesy
> This *fawning greyhound* then did offer me,

and in *Hamlet*—

> Let the *candied tongue* lick absurd pomp
> And crook the pregnant hinges of the knee
> Where thrift may follow *fawning*.

These two quotations taken in conjunction with the example in *Julius Caesar* show how " the hearts that spaniel'd me at heels " in *Antony and Cleopatra* suggested " discandy, melt their sweets ". Dogs were always present at the Elizabethan table and licked the hand of the guests, fawning and begging for the candied sweetmeats.

But in the main Shakespeare follows the direct manner of North's *Plutarch*. Two sentences in that narrative are worth noticing: " Antonius thinking . . . his body should be honourably buried, and not in hugger-mugger ". This must have suggested, " We have done but greenly in hugger-mugger to inter him " (*Hamlet*, IV. 5. 84), and links the two plays. Also in the same passage in North we have, " He

framed his eloquence to make their hearts yearn ";
and this probably accounts for the recurrence of the
word at this period; in *Julius Caesar* itself—

> That every like is not the same, O Caesar,
> The heart of Brutus yearns to think upon.

In *The Merry Wives*—

> She laments, sir, for it, that it would yearn your heart to see,

and *three times* in *Henry V*. (the same year as *Julius
Caesar*)—

> My manly heart doth yearn.
>
> Falstaff he is dead, and we must yearn therefore.
>
> It yearns me not if men my garments wear.

There is only one other instance in Shakespeare. The
word has in our own time lost this meaning—" to
grieve ".

The style of *Hamlet* differs from that of *Julius
Caesar* as champagne does from ale. *Hamlet* is the
longest of Shakespeare's plays, the plot is the most
exciting, the most elaborate, and, outside *Antony and
Cleopatra*, the most episodic. As we have seen, there
is a very strong proportion of prose. All these things
combine to make it seem in reading the richest of the
plays; but that richness is, as a matter of fact, exemplified yet further in the actual style. In *Hamlet*,
Shakespeare again and again uses two words where
one would do. Always, he is phrase-making. In the
following he employs the double noun:

" The gross and scope of my opinion ", " covenant

and carriage of the article ", " the trappings and the suits of woe ", " the dead vast and middle of the night ", " a fashion and a toy in blood ", " the shot and danger of desire ", " the morn and liquid dew of youth ", " the pith and marrow of our attribute ", " the pales and forts of reason ", " gates and alleys of the body ", " the book and volume of my brain ", " encompassment and drift of question ", " the supply and profit of our hope ", " the slings and arrows of outrageous fortune ", " the motive and the cue for passion " " the origin and commencement of his grief ", " the teeth and forehead of our faults ", " proof and bulwark against sense ", " the grace and blush of modesty ", " the heat and flame of thy distemper ", " strength and armour of the mind ", " the ratifiers and props of every word ", " the brooch and gem of all the nation ", " a voice and precedent of peace ", " enterprises of great pith and moment ", " circumstance and course of thought ", " the expectancy and rose of the fair state ".

Here one must pause, for we have lighted upon one of the most unique and most important of characteristics in Shakespeare's style.

Sir Walter Raleigh in his *Shakespeare*, quotes Gray's dictum—" Every word with him is a picture " —and selects a few examples, such as " a malignant and a turbaned Turk ", " Even in the force and road of casuality ". Now it is the aim of the poet, in his word combinations, to make each one ring the clearest possible note, without destroying the harmony. And a familiar method—Sir Thomas Browne was a master of it—is the use of contrast, of putting concrete up against abstract, the native element beside the foreign and monosyllable to set off polysyllable. Shakespeare began quite early to favour the abstract and concrete combination, amplifying one noun with two others, employing a current and pictorial word, making his readers see as well as think.

Here are some of the earlier examples. " Aged contusions and all brush of time ", " the silver livery of advised age ", " and in thy reverence and chair-days thus ", " the eye and prospect of your town ", " the grappling vigour and rough frown of war ", " the thorns and dangers of this world ", " the chaff and ruin of the times ", " the quality and hair of the attempt brook no division ", " the dove and very blessed spirit of peace ", " with casted slough and fresh legerity ", " the quick forge and working house of thought ", " and silken dalliance in the wardrobe lies ". These last three remarkable pieces of phrasing belong to *Henry V.*, the play which seems to close one period and inaugurate another. But it is in *Hamlet* that these amplifications are employed with such surprising profusion. I have quoted above no less than twenty-seven uses, some of which, so natural is it to the author to fall into the mode, verge on the tautological (*e.g.* " heat and flame of thy distemper ", " the brooch and gem of all the nation "); even so I have not exhausted them. *All's Well*, *Troilus and Cressida* and *Measure for Measure* provide instances: " the catastrophe and heel of pastime ", " the staggers and the careless lapse of youth and ignorance ", " husks and formless ruin of oblivion ", " the fault and glimpse of newness ", " the tooth of time and razure of oblivion ". In *Othello* we still have the same trick of speech, although with less frequency: " a flag and sign of love ", " the head and front of my offending ", " downright violence and storm of fortunes ", " recognisance and pledge of love ", " the shot of accident nor dart of chance ", " forms and visages of duty ". But the style is more winnowed than that of *Hamlet*. In the later plays the examples are few and more elaborate; metaphor is differently employed. Here are some extensions of the same thing: " the bellows and the fan to cool a gipsy's lust " (a double idea paradoxically combined), " the voice of occupation and the breath of garliceaters ", " the dark backward and abysm of time ".

We must now take up again the style of *Hamlet*, of which these amplifications are a peculiar feature. They have obviously an affinity with Euphuism; but the use of metaphor is distinct from that which Shakespeare developed in his mature style, namely, as a chain to link together ideas and dialogue even, a guiding thread in the intricate windings of his thought. No less noticeable is the profusion of adjectives, which cluster round the substantives in twos and threes. Young poets, especially when they are writing to order and against time, use adjectives to fill up gaps. Shakespeare is no exception. In the *Comedy of Errors* we frequently meet with the familiar combination of two epithets and two nouns. In the first scene, for example:

> A joyful mother of two goodly sons.
> And piteous plainings of two pretty babes.

> A doubtful warrant of immediate death.
> Gave healthful welcome to their shipwrack'd guests.

In the historical plays the padding often takes the form of wretched double forms—*blood-drinking sighs, earnest-gaping sight, furnace-burning heart, water-standing eye, dead-killing news.* So also in the *Venus and Adonis,* in the very first stanza we have *purple-coloured, rose-cheeked, sick-thoughted, bold-faced,* and elsewhere the less decorative *life-poisoning, well-breath'd, marrow-eating, grim-grinning.*[1] Shakespeare has a large vocabulary of epithets, and in his early work he uses them either poetically or as a makeshift to piece out the line. In *Richard III.* he begins to accumulate them rhetorically; witness the first thirty lines of the play. Their character becomes more interesting: "key-cold figure", "creeping, venomed thing", "elvish-marked, abortive, rooting hog", "empty, vast and wandering air", "flaky darkness", "blind cave of eternal night". In the writing of *Romeo and Juliet,* the adjective plays an important part—

> Come, civil night,
> Thou sober-suited matron, all in black,

and even where the tragedy should have control over the poetry—

> O, here
> Will I set up my everlasting rest
> And shake the yoke of inauspicious stars
> From this world-wearied flesh. Eyes, look your last,
> Arms, take your last embrace! and lips, O you
> The doors of breath, seal with a righteous kiss
> A dateless bargain to engrossing death.

[1] Spenser and Sidney learnt the double epithet from the practice and precept of the Pléiade.

> Come, bitter conduct, come unsavoury guide!
> Thou desperate pilot, now at once run on
> The dashing rocks thy sea-sick weary bark!

The adjectives, selected with equal care for their meaning and sound, are doing half the work.

In *King John* and 1 and 2 *Henry IV*. they are much more digested, except for an occasional moment when he throws his cap at the sublime.

> Death, death; O, amiable lovely death!
> Thou odoriferous stench! sound rottenness!
> Arise forth from the couch of lasting night,
> Thou hate and terror to prosperity,
> And I will kiss thy detestable bones,
> And put my eyeballs in thy vaulty brows,
> And ring these fingers with thy household worms,
> And stop this gap of breath with fulsome dust.

In *Henry V.*, however, they again rise to the surface. They run in pairs, sometimes alliterative: *fatal and neglected English, invisible and creeping wind, culled and choice-drawn cavaliers, blind and bloody soldier, weary and all-watched night, rough and all-unable pen, creeping murmur and the poring dark, hot and forcing violation, high-upreared and abutting fronts, his bruised helmet and his bended sword, scambling and unquiet time, sweet and honeyed sentences, swelling scene, nook-shotten isle, wild and wasteful ocean.* And then, with *Hamlet*, comes the deluge. In that rich and redundant style adjectives, verbs and nouns climb on each other's shoulders. Every word has an understudy, as it were. A few instances will suffice: *delicate and tender prince, a loving and a fair reply, puff'd and reckless libertine, ponderous and marble jaws, deject and wretched, a dull and muddy-mettled rascal, knotted and combined locks, wild and whirling words, steep and thorny way, noble and most sovereign reason, oppress'd and fear-surprised eyes, sensible and true avouch, trivial fond records*; or take Gertrude's description of Ophelia's death, or the Ghost's speech in I. 5, with such a passage as this:

> Upon my *secure* hour thy uncle stole,
> With juice of *cursed* hebona in a vial,
> And in the porches of my ear did pour
> The *leperous* distilment; whose effect
> Holds such an enmity with blood of man
> That *swift* as quicksilver it courses through
> The *natural* gates and alleys of the body,
> And with a *sudden* vigour it doth posset
> And curd, like *eager* droppings into milk,
> The *thin* and *wholesome* blood; so did it mine;
> And a most *instant* tetter bark'd about,
> Most *lazar-like*, with *vile* and *loathsome* crust
> All my *smooth* body.

A *crescendo* of original and telling epithets.

In *Hamlet* the Latin element, of which we have spoken, makes itself felt. To select one word—

> There, on the *pendent* boughs her coronet weeds
> Clambering to hang,

which is also found in *Measure for Measure*, " the pendent world "; in *Macbeth*, " his pendent bed and procreant cradle "; in *Antony and Cleopatra*, " a tower'd citadel, a pendent rock ".

Here also we have the first sublime example of the Latin diction, perhaps the best in all the plays—

> Absent thee from felicity awhile

which is succeeded by tolling native monosyllables——

> And in this harsh world draw thy breath in pain.

Felicity only occurs in one other place, in the embellished comedy *Love's Labour's Lost*, which flirts and fools with Latin formations.

We may note, by the way, that Polonius's pompous "Perpend" took Shakespeare's fancy at this date. It occurs in *The Merry Wives*, *As You Like It*, *Twelfth Night* and *Henry V.* (1599–1600) and never again, on each occasion with a twinkle in the eye.

It is in *Hamlet* also that "sulphur" and "sulphurous" first appear, which took Shakespeare's imagination in the later plays. The occasions are worth tabulating: the Ghost says——

> My hour is almost come
> When I to sulphurous and tormenting flames
> Must render up myself.

Iago utters the menacing truth——

> Dangerous conceits are in their natures poisons,
> Which at the first are scarce found to distaste,
> But with a little act upon the blood,
> Burn like the mines of sulphur;

and in the same play we have——

> Roast me in sulphur,
> Wash me in steep-down gulfs of liquid fire,

and in *Lear*——

> There's hell, there's darkness, there's the sulphurous pit
> Burning, scalding.

These all go together; the other seven examples are all concerned with the lightning.

All's Well That Ends Well.—This is a crippled unrewarding play. The frequent use of the couplet (Helen and the King have nearly a hundred lines of them in one scene), the quatrains at I. 3. 136, the sonnet letter, are evidence for an early date. And in the main the style is as direct as in *The Merchant of Venice*. The abundance of prose, even in the mouths of the serious characters, points to the transitional period at the close of the century. Possibly Shakespeare worked upon an older piece, more probably he worked upon the play at two different dates. For we have symptoms of the mature style. Lines 71-117 in the first scene, the second scene in the first Act, and the last scene in the play, show the new command of language and metre. There are also links with *Hamlet*. In scene 1 the Countess's farewell to Bertram is a close parallel with that of Polonius to Laertes—

> Love all, trust a few,
> Do wrong to none; be able for thine enemy
> Rather in power than use, and keep thy friend
> Under thy own life's key; be check'd for silence
> But never tax'd for speech.

A few lines further down we have " collateral " which occurs in *Hamlet* and not elsewhere. Then—

> 'Twas pretty, though a plague,
> To see him every hour; to sit and draw
> His arched brows, his hawking eye, his curls,
> In our heart's table; heart too capable
> Of every line and trick of his sweet favour.
> But now he's gone, and my idolatrous fancy
> Must sanctify his reliques.

which is slight beside—

> Look here upon this picture and on this,
> The counterfeit presentment of two brothers;
> See, what a grace was seated on this brow,
> Hyperion's curls, the front of Jove himself,
> An eye like Mars to threaten and command . . .

but of the same design; the first in pencil, the second in oils.   Act I. 2 was undoubtedly written in or after 1600; it is in the new manner.   Here for instance we have a few Latinisms (otherwise rare in this play): *prejudicates*, *demonstrate*, *plausive* (otherwise only in *Hamlet*, and *unplausive* in *Troilus and Cressida*), *credible* (once in Shakespeare), *credence* (only in *Troilus and Cressida*; we find *credent* in *Hamlet*, *Measure for Measure* and *The Winter's Tale*).   Here also is the astonishing phrase " catastrophe and heel of pastime "; and the metaphor which follows—

> Let me not live, quoth he,
> After my flame lacks oil to be the snuff
> Of younger spirits,

recalls in *Hamlet*—

> There lives within the very flame of love
> A kind of wick or snuff that will abate it.

The last scene of all smacks somewhat of the mature style; for instance—

> Natural rebellion done *i' the* blaze of youth
> When oil and fire too strong for reason's force
> O'erbears it and burns on;

and this passage—

> he lost a wife
> Whose beauty did astonish the survey
> Of richest eyes, whose words all ears took captive,
> Whose dear perfections hearts that scorn'd to serve
> Humbly call'd mistress;

which recalls some of the cadences of Troilus in Priam's council chamber.

> He brought a Grecian queen whose youth and freshness
> Wrinkles Apollo's and makes stale the morning.
> Is she worth keeping?   Why, she is a pearl
> Whose price hath launch'd above a thousand ships
> And turn'd crown'd kings to merchants.

At line 41 we come upon a phrase which must be the occasion for another diversion, " the *inaudible and noiseless* foot of time ".   Of the pairing of epithets in Shakespeare I have already spoken; I have emphasised the significance of his experiments in verbal contrasts, particularly those in which the abstract and the concrete are yoked together, such as " my snuff and loathed part of nature " (*King Lear*).   Thirdly, the invasion of Latin words has been espied.   In " the inaudible and noiseless foot of time " we have yet another Shakespearian trick which has an affinity with all these three.   We have some quite early examples; but most of them belong to the period between *Henry V*. and *Macbeth*.   I select these—

> Inestimable stones, unvalued jewels.
>
> Exterior form, outward accoutrement.
>
> In his bright radiance and collateral light.
>
> Thou odoriferous stench, sound rottenness.
>
> Affliction is enamoured of thy parts
> And thou art wedded to calamity.

> Since nor the exterior nor the inward man.
>
> O insupportable and touching loss.
>
> Irreparable is the loss, and patience
> Says it is past her cure.
>
> 'Tis no sinister nor no awkward claim.

" Infinite and boundless reach ", " an infinite and endless liar ", " indign and base adversities ", " impotent and snail-paced beggary ", " invisible and creeping wind ", " corresponsive and fulfilling bolts ", " extravagant and erring spirit ", " extravagant and wheeling stranger ", " exsufflicate and blown surmises ", " earthy and abhorred commands ".

It is in *Troilus and Cressida* that the Latin vocabulary begins to unbalance if not to play havoc with the style. The following is a typical passage—

> Sith yet there is a credence in my heart,
> An esperance so obstinately strong,
> That doth invert the attest of eyes and ears,
> As if those organs had deceptious functions,
> Created only to calumniate.

In diction this more resembles the thews and sinews of the late tragedies and final plays, but not in metre and syntax. The Latin polysyllables which make *Troilus and Cressida* unique in style among Shakespeare's plays make up a formidable and astonishing list: *propugnation, expostulation, sequent protestation, maculation, remuneration, recordation, speculation, cognition, erudition, dexterity, consanguinity, taciturnity, turpitude,*

conflux, conjecture, oppugnancy, sanctimony, assubjugate,
devolve, divert, celerity, propension, priority, refractory,
scurril, deject, vindicative, tortive and errant, prenominate,
mirable, multipotent, dexter, laud, sinister, corresponsive,
deracinate, protractive, exasperate, emulation, fractions,
conduce, diminutive, propend, portable, negation, convive.

The introduction of the Latin element which made
Shakespeare's style at once more abstract and more
intellectual, left its mark also upon the *Sonnets*. From
the obscure No. 107, which seems to refer to the
succession of James, to No. 125, which except for
the *envoi* (126) closes the main body of the sonnets,
we have clear signs of the new diction. Moreover,
the expression is subdued to the thought. Canon
Beeching was the first to note the affinity between the
later sonnets and the style of *Troilus and Cressida.*

> Never believe . . .
> That it could so preposterously be stained.   (109)
>
> In so profound abysm I throw all care
> Of other's voices, that my adder's sense
> To critic and to flatterer stopped are.
> Mark how with my neglect I do dispense.   (112)
>
> Since I left you, mine eye is in my mind;
> And that which governs me to go about
> Doth part his function and is partly blind,
> Seems seeing but effectually is out.   (113)
>
> Incapable of more, replete with you.   (113)
>
> Let me not to the marriage of true minds
> Admit impediments.   Love is not love
> Which alters when it alteration finds.   (116)
>
> That I have frequent been with unknown minds.   (117)
>
> And on just proof surmise accumulate.   (117)

> Thus policy in love, to anticipate
> The ills that were not, grew to faults assured,
> And brought to medicine a healthful state
> Which, rank of goodness, would by ill be cured.   (118)

> With my extern the outward honouring.   (125)

> No, let me be obsequious in thy heart,
> And take thou my oblation, poor but free.   (125)

And in 122 *faculty*, *subsist*, *oblivion*, *retention*, *adjunct*, *import*.

The style of *Troilus and Cressida* is similar to that of *Hamlet*, but in advance of it.   There is the same system of double-phrasing, the same frequency of epithet, the same accumulations, the same use of prose and of broken lines.   Thus we have " envious fever of pale and bloodless emulation ", " ridiculous and awkward action ", " lamp and flames of love ", " negligent and loose regard ", " the sinew and the forehand of our host ", " cause and question ", " base and building of my love ", " her base and pillar ", " shapes and forms of slaughter ", " dull and factious nobles ", " push and enmity ", " fan and wind of your fair sword ", etc.   The climaxes, as in *Hamlet*, are usually achieved by piling term upon term, which has been noted in a previous chapter as characteristic of the earlier manner, but never entirely abandoned.

> How could communities,
> Degrees in schools and brotherhoods in cities,
> Peaceful commerce from dividable shores,
> The primogenitive and due of birth,
> Prerogative of age, crowns, sceptres, laurels
> But by degree, stand in authentic place?

and

> All our abilities, gifts, natures, shapes,
> Severals and generals of grace exact,
> Achievements, plots, orders, preventions,
> Excitements to the field, or speech for truce,
> Success or loss, what is or is not, serves
> As stuff for these two to make paradoxes;

and

> For beauty, wit,
> High birth, vigour of bone, desert in service,
> Love, friendship, charity are subjects all
> To envious and calumniating time;

and

> The fractions of her faith, orts of her love,
> The fragments, scraps, the bits and greasy reliques
> Of her o'er-eaten faith.

But the metaphors in *Troilus and Cressida* are differently employed to those in *Hamlet*; they illuminate the thought instead of inlaying the diction. The metaphors of Ulysses and Nestor swell into similes. They unwind their coils from line to line; and it is in this respect that the style leaves *Hamlet* behind and looks on to *Macbeth*.

> the seeded pride
> That hath to this maturity blown up
> In rank Achilles, must or now be cropp'd
> Or, shedding, breed a nursery of like evil
> To overbulk us all.

> And in such indexes, although small pricks
> To their subsequent volumes, there is seen
> The baby figure of the giant mass
> Of things to come at large.

O

> Take the instant way;
> For honour travels in a strait so narrow
> Where one but goes abreast; keep then the path;
> For emulation hath a thousand sons
> That one by one pursue; if you give way,
> Or hedge aside from the direct forthright,
> Like to an enter'd tide they all rush by
> And leave you hindmost.

Although in this play Shakespeare cracks the bonds of his vocabulary and appropriates so much that is new, yet from now on his diction is " subdued to what it works in, like the dyer's hand ", that is, to the thought.

Shakespeare's experience in the English history plays reaps a rich harvest in the council scenes of Priam and Agamemnon.   In the first part of *Henry IV.* the dispute between Hotspur and Glendower gives life to the scene, but there is nothing in this or in the second part to compare with the characterisation and variety of speed in the corresponding type in *Troilus and Cressida*.   The tediousness of Nestor, the decision of Ulysses, the enthusiasm of Troilus, the nerveless sentiment of Paris, the elder-brotherliness of Hector, all these are admirable and succeed in carrying the lengthy static scenes and in endowing them with internal action.   In strong contrast to these we find in V. 2 a scene written entirely for the stage; as in *Hamlet*, we have a play within a play.   Ulysses, the hard-headed and middle-aged, and Troilus, who breathes all the illusions of first love, witness the encounter between Cressida and the lecherous Diomed, while Thersites acts as chorus.   Thus three separate conversations, or, rather, two dialogues and a soliloquy, are carried on simultaneously. It is a masterly piece of dramatic writing which acts better than it reads, a rare thing in Shakespeare.

I am not convinced that *Troilus and Cressida* (like *All's Well*) is the work of two different dates, nor that there are signs of substantial revision. Probably, like *Hamlet*, Shakespeare had it on his desk for some time, and, moreover, during a transitional period when his style was in the melting-pot. Certainly the great Ulysses speech, " Time hath, my lord, a wallet on his back ", seems in advance of the rest of the play. But a false impression arises from the lack of unity in the play. The hero and heroine of the title hold a very much less central position than Antony and Cleopatra, just as Achilles is a far more important figure than Octavius Caesar. The Palace of Priam and the Grecian Camp are presented with equal fullness and joined by a double strand of plot, the Ajax-Achilles-Hector tragedy and the Troilus-Cressida-Diomed tragedy. The tragedy of war, which is concerned with the pride and policy of warriors and statesmen, demands one atmosphere, the tragedy of first love another. Thersites in the first corresponds to Pandarus in the second and through their mouths the same lesson is enforced. But as there are two atmospheres, so there are two styles. And in this play Shakespeare achieves another success, in that every speech is extraordinarily suited to the character of the speaker. Cressida speaks prose and couplets, Troilus slips easily into pure poetry, Ulysses is intellectual and his words

instinct with thought.   How clearly Shakespeare had
the characters of his persons in his mind's eye may be
seen in Act IV. 5, in which the Grecians, after the duel,
pay their greetings to Hector and at last Achilles meets
him face to face.   Again the style of Act II. 2 is
different from I. 3, because the sons of Priam are
different from the Greek commanders.   This is a
great improvement upon the English history plays in
which only an occasional figure like Hotspur stands
out from the tapestry background of the council scenes.

The movement of the verse is closely akin to that
of *Hamlet*.   Read, for example, Laertes's farewell to
Ophelia, or the speech of Claudius, "'Tis sweet and
commendable in thy nature, Hamlet", containing
such a passage as this—

> Fie! 'tis a fault to heaven,
> A fault against the dead, a fault to nature,
> To reason most absurd, whose common theme
> Is death of fathers, and who still hath cried,
> From the first corse till he that died to-day,
> "This must be so",

and then compare with them *Troilus and Cressida*, II. 2,
noting especially—

> If you'll avouch 'twas reason Paris went—
> As you must needs, for you all cried " Go, go "—
> If you'll confess he brought home noble prize—
> As you must needs, for you all clapped your hands,
> And cried " Inestimable! " . . .

and

> Fie, fie! my brother,
> Weigh you the worth and honour of a king
> So great as our dread father in a scale

> Of common ounces? will you with counters sum
> The past proportion of his infinite?
> And buckle in a waist most fathomless
> With spans and inches so diminutive
> As fears and reasons? fie, for godly shame!

and Hector's summing up.

Then such a sentence as—

> They clepe us drunkards, and with swinish phrase
> Soil our addition;

points in style to *Troilus and Cressida*. This particular use of *addition* is common in the later plays of Shakespeare and occurs *four times* in our play.

> I came to kill thee, cousin, and bear hence
> A great addition.

It is my belief that *Troilus* followed *Hamlet* by more than a year, and it is quite likely that the revision of *All's Well* may have been later still, despite the suggestions of *Hamlet* in scene I. 1. At any rate we have in scene I. 2 of *All's Well* three remarkable light endings:

>   he did look far
> Into the service of the time, and was
> Discipled of the bravest.

>   his honour,
> Clock to itself, knew the true minute when
> Exception bid him speak.

> Of younger spirits, whose apprehensive senses
> All but new things disdain; whose judgements are
> Mere fathers of their garments.

The more one reads the scene the more one is tempted to push it forward to the end of the Central Period and

the beginning of the final style.   In Act II. 1 we have
the even more startling—

> When our most learned doctors leave us, and
> The congregated college have concluded. . . .

These endings are not found in *Hamlet* or *Othello*.   At
line 128 we go back to the old play, but the earlier part
of the scene provides " Bring in the admiration ",
which is typical of the latest style.   Parolles says " a
more *dilated* farewell " (cp. *spacious and dilated parts*,
Troilus and Cressida), and Lafeu, " I am Cressid's uncle,
that dare leave two together ".   Altogether the question
of date is a most puzzling one; it is not rash to suppose
that we have the work of three different periods and
that the *Love's Labour's Won* of Meres's list was twice
revised by Shakespeare, in 1600 and again four or five
years later.

Measure for Measure is the last of the mixed, baffling
plays, the last in which the extremities of good and bad
excel themselves.   For in *Timon* and in *Pericles* we
follow Mr. Dugdale Sykes and can distinguish another
hand.   *Measure for Measure*, like *All's Well* and
Troilus, has many of the characteristics of *Hamlet*, and
all these four experiment in diction, in the new use of
metaphor and amplification, in Latinising the vocabulary.
In the tragedies which succeed *Measure for Measure*,
the speeches are more closely fitted to the character of
the speakers and to the situation.

In this play, apart from the rich comedy of Pompey,
Abhorson and Barnadine and the inconsistent irre-
pressible Lucio, there is little characterisation.   Shake-

speare concentrates on Angelo, preparing dramatically
for his first entrance, and treating him like Hamlet and
Brutus as a study in conflict with the aid of soliloquy.

I will select a few small points that are worth
attention.   In connection with the double-phrasing
already examined, we note " a leavened and prepared
choice ", " drowsy and neglected art ", " a prone
and speechless dialect ", " all nicety and prolixious
blushes ", " stroke and line of his great justice ",
" a purpose more grave and wrinkled ".   More
important is the Duke's sermon to Claudio, " Be
absolute for death " (III. 1), which is in style the
exact counterpart of Ulysses's " Time hath, my lord,
a wallet at his back ".   In both the thought guides
the language, and metaphor is employed for reasoning,
not for ornament.   Compare, for instance, with the
Troilus and Cressida speech such extracts as these:

> Merely, thou art death's fool;
> For him thou labour'st by thy flight to shun,
> And yet run'st toward him still.   Thou art not noble;
> For all th' accommodations that thou bear'st
> Are nursed by baseness.

> If thou art rich, thou'rt poor;
> For, like an ass whose back with ingots bows,
> Thou bear'st thy heavy riches but a journey,
> And death unloads thee.

> Thou hast nor youth nor age;
> But, as it were, an after-dinner's sleep,
> Dreaming on both; for all thy blessed youth
> Becomes as aged, and doth beg the alms
> Of palsied eld; and when thou art old and rich,
> Thou hast neither heat, affection, limb, nor beauty
> To make thy riches pleasant. . . .

The metre does not cramp, it hardly affects the speaker;
but it is significant that in thirty-seven lines we have nine-
teen strong pauses in the middle instead of the end of the
line; it has become the natural place in which to begin
and close a sentence, a great advance upon *Hamlet*.

Another example of the reasoning style is to be
found in II. 1:

> 'Tis very pregnant,
> The jewel that we find, we stoop and take it
> Because we see it; but what we do not see
> We tread upon, and never think of it.
> You may not so extenuate his offence,
> For I have had such faults.

This is in the manner of Iago:

> Good name in man and woman, dear my lord,
> Is the immediate jewel of their souls;
> Who steals my purse steals trash; 'tis something, nothing;
> 'Twas mine, 'tis his, and has been slave to thousands;
> But he that filches from me my good name
> Robs me of that which not enriches him,
> And makes me poor indeed.

Iago and Ulysses are of the same intellectual metal, and
a vein of it is to be found in *Measure for Measure*.

Angelo's *pregnant* has already occurred in I. 1.
The first appearance of the word is in *Twelfth Night*,
where it is much admired by Sir Andrew, and in the
tragedies it becomes a metaphorical favourite of
Shakespeare's, in *Hamlet*, *Troilus*, *Othello*, *Lear*, *Timon*,
Antony, *Cymbeline* and *The Winter's Tale*, including
some curious uses: *e.g.* "the pregnant hinges of the
knee", "pregnant and potential spurs", "pregnant to

good pity", "pregnant instrument of wrath"; examples of his happy ruthlessness with words.

Another new metaphor occurs twice:

> There is our commission
> From which we would not have you warp,

and " such a warped slip of wilderness ". The word is used twice in *As You Like It*, but not metaphorically. We have, however, in *All's Well*—

> Contempt his scornful perspective did lend me
> Which warped the line of every other favour.

Lear has "warp'd looks", and *The Winter's Tale*, "my favour here begins to warp ". The *Measure for Measure* passage above is typical of Shakespeare's practice of rejecting the natural and obvious word in preference for one more vivid and powerful, although less familiar. For instance, in this same play—

> It was the swift celerity of his death
> Which I did think with slower foot came on
> That *brain'd* my purpose.

On the other hand, " swift celerity " shows that Shakespeare used his new Latinisms for their own sake, for sound and novelty, more than for their sense.

The most terrific line in the play is, of course, the famous—

> To lie in cold obstruction and to rot.

What a combination of abstract and concrete! The vague formidable phrase — I have heard its exact meaning discussed with acrimony — is brought up against a pitiless monosyllable.   It is one of the best examples of a favourite Shakespearian device.

Othello, *King Lear* and *Macbeth* complete the Central Period.   In all three the style is in harmony with the atmosphere; that is to say, the diction holds the correct relation to the other dramatic elements and is less independent than in Shakespeare's other work.

Othello has the Sophoclean perfection, the *aurea mediocritas* of writing.   Thus the Moor's apologia and story of his courtship—

> Her father loved me; oft invited me,
> Still questioned me the story of my life
> From year to year, the battles, sieges, fortunes
> That I have passed . . .

is in syntax, versification and use of words one of the most natural and convincing things in Shakespeare, and yet is far more subtle than the prose use of verse already noted in *The Merchant of Venice*.

The speeches are in character; Cassio's enthusiasm (he reminds me of Troilus), the simplicity of Desdemona, the smutty mind of Iago, all these are revealed in their words.   Bradley has written well on Othello's romantic make-up and the poetry of his speech. Shakespeare in his borrowings from Philemon Holland's translation of Pliny employed a favourite method of Elizabethan and Jacobean dramatists, of Webster and of Donne, but unlike them he puts these fables and traveller's tales into the mouth of the Moor, with the deliberate intent of throwing a romantic colouring over his hero, not for their own sake.   The base Indian, the sybil in her prophetic fury, the Pontick sea with icy current and compulsive course, the Arabian trees dropping their medicinable gum, the turbaned Turk, the Anthropophagi, and such little touches as " some nine moons wasted ", " aspics' tongues ", " a sword of Spain, the icebrook's temper ", " one entire and perfect chrysolite " — all these are to *Othello* what the elements are to *Lear* and the witches to *Macbeth*. It is a new experiment on Shakespeare's part.

Similarly in *Lear* there are no generalisations to be made about the diction and style; the peculiar effect of the play is produced by the characters and situation, by throwing together the Fool, Edgar and the King— or rather the Fool, the mock-madman and an old man toppling on the verge of madness; by combining prose and verse, tragedy and comedy, and interchanging superstition, philosophy, curses, scraps of popular airs and dirty jokes. There are, however, three small points which strike me.

The first is the way in which comparisons and images are drawn from the animal world.

Thus Gloucester's " Unnatural, debased, brutish villain! worse than brutish. . . . He cannot be such a monster ", and Edmund's ironic " An admirable evasion of whoremaster man, to lay his goatish disposition to the charge of a star! My father compounded with my mother under the dragon's tail, and my nativity was under *ursa major*; so that it follows, I am rough and lecherous." Then with Lear and his daughters—

Ingratitude, thou marble-hearted fiend,
More hideous when thou show'st thee in a child
Than the sea-monster!

How sharper than a serpent's tooth it is
To have a thankless child.

When she shall hear this of thee, with her nails
She'll flay thy wolvish visage.

O Regan, she hath tied
Sharp-toothed unkindness, like a vulture, here.

struck me with her tongue
Most serpent-like, upon the very heart.

Filial ingratitude!
Is it not as this mouth should tear this hand
For lifting food to 't.

'twas this flesh begot
Those pelican daughters.

Now, you she-foxes.

Because I would not see thy cruel nails
Pluck out his poor old eyes; nor thy fierce sister
In his anointed flesh stick boorish fangs.

Tigers, not daughters, what have you performed?

Humanity must perforce prey on itself,
Like monsters of the deep.

The fitchew nor the soiled horse goes to 't
With a more riotous appetite.
Down from the waist they are Centaurs,
Though women all above;

and " detested kite ", " this gilded serpent ", " dog-hearted daughters ", " toad-spotted traitor ", and of Oswald—

Such smiling rogues as these,
Like rats, oft bite the holy cords a-twain
That are too intrinse t' unloose.

Add to these the quips of the Fool, such as—

> The hedge-sparrow fed the cuckoo so long
> That it had it head bit off by it young.

These are all heightened even further by a reverse application; thus:

> mine enemy's dog,
> Though he had bit me, should have stood that night
> Against my fire,

and

> A father, and a gracious aged man,
> Whose reverence the head-lugged bear would lick,

and

> Why should a dog, a horse, a rat, have life,
> And thou no breath at all?

and the King's being turned out " to be a comrade with the wolf and owl ", on a night

> wherein the cub-drawn bear would couch,
> The lion and the belly-pinched wolf
> Keep their fur dry.

The cumulative effect of the bestial analogies throughout the play is ironic and sinister. What an advance in subtlety on the proverbial and euphuistic uses in the earlier plays, the " dove-feathered raven, wolfish-ravening lamb " of *Romeo and Juliet*, or " who scapes the lurking serpent's mortal sting " (3 *Henry VI.*).

Secondly, in *Lear*, as in *Timon*, the forces of nature do not merely supply the background before and in the midst of which the conflict and catastrophe take place. There is the same insistence upon the winds and waters, the thunder and lightning, the cataracts and hurricanes,

as there is in *Macbeth* upon blood and darkness. This
particularly distinguishes the play from its predecessor.
Othello's thoughts in his agony turn to the plumed
troop, the neighing steed, the royal banner, the ear-
piercing fife; all his feelings centre round Desdemona
and his own romantic life. But the appeals of Lear
are to the heavens. He ranges himself with the
elements. His cries and curses invoke nature.

> Hear, Nature, hear! dear goddess, hear!
> Suspend thy purpose, if thou didst intend
> To make this creature fruitful!

> And thou, all-shaking thunder,
> Strike flat the thick rotundity o' the world,
> Crack nature's moulds, all germens spill at once,
> That make ingrateful man!

How different this is from—

> Yet she must die or she'll betray more men.

Add to these—

> O heavens,
> If you do love old men, if your sweet sway
> Allow obedience, if yourselves are old,
> Make it your cause; send down, and take my part!

and

> You nimble lightnings, dart your blinding flames
> Into her scornful eyes!

and

> O ruined piece of nature! This great world
> Shall so wear out to nought.

Thirdly, I note the number of detached and con-
centrated γνῶμαι, final utterances of a still small voice

that rises above the strife and storm, and, like the Greek chorus, give the conclusion of the whole matter. Poetry, says the axiom, expresses the universal. And these are in harmony with the atmosphere of the play:

> The art of our necessities is strange
> That can make vile things precious.

> It is the stars,
> The stars above us govern our conditions.

> Men must endure
> Their going hence even as their coming hither.
> Ripeness is all.

> As flies to wanton boys are we to the gods;
> They kill us for their sport.

> The gods are just, and of our pleasant vices
> Make instruments to plague us.

> The wheel is come full circle; I am here.

> O, our lives' sweetness!
> That we the pain of death would hourly die
> Rather than die at once!

In *Lear* we have the conflicting principles of tragedy, the two-edged philosophy of life.

The atmosphere of *Macbeth* has been minutely considered and luminously expounded by Bradley; the style is more violent and more rapid than that of *Lear*. It is no less individual than the two plays it follows and the character is still in command of the diction. The neurotic imagination of Macbeth is given free rein, and the unyielding matter-of-factness of the Queen is so savagely emphasised that, in view of her collapse after the murder, one is tempted to

believe that she was from the first conscious of a
flaw, a secret terror, and bolstered herself up with
murderous protestations.

Macbeth is the most metaphorical of the plays.
The metaphor is not used for hendiadys as in Hamlet,
but to develop and unwind the thought. We have
already noted symptoms of this method as early as
Julius Caesar and later in *Troilus and Cressida*. But
in *Macbeth* Shakespeare's intellect leaps nimble as
lightning from one metaphor to another. They are
not common in *King Lear*: when Albany says—

> She that herself will sliver and disbranch
> From her material sap, perforce must wither
> And come to deadly use,

Goneril is impatient at the frigidity of manner and
retorts—

> No more; the text is foolish.

With *Macbeth* comes more speed, more heat. Our
very familiarity with the play may perhaps blind us
to the extraordinary accumulations and combinations
of metaphors and must serve here as an excuse for
quoting what is too well known.

Here, first, are some single metaphors, some of
them mannered in style. Three follow one another
in thirty lines:

> two truths are told
> As happy prologues to the swelling act
> Of the imperial theme.

> New honours come upon him,
> Like our strange garments; cleave not to their mould
> But with the aid of use.

> Kind gentlemen, your pains
> Are registered where every day I turn
> The leaf to read them.

Lady Macbeth has a similar metaphor to this last:

> Your face, my thane, is as a book where men
> May read strange matters.

These can be paralleled in the earlier plays; more unique are—

> Most sacrilegious murder has broke ope
> The Lord's anointed temple and stole thence
> The life o' the building,

which is repeated in *Cymbeline*—

> I am Posthumus
> That killed thy daughter; villain-like I lie;
> That caused a lesser villain than myself,
> A sacrilegious thief, to do't; the temple
> Of virtue was she,

and

> The wine of life is drawn; and the mere lees
> Is left this vault to brag of,

and

> in his commendations I am fed;
> It is a banquet to me.

Here on the other hand are several thrown together:

> For them the gracious Duncan have I murdered;
> Put rancours in the vessel of my peace
> Only for them; and my eternal jewel
> Given to the common enemy of man,
> To make them kings, the seed of Banquo kings!
> Rather than so, come fate into the list
> And champion me to the utterance!

P

and

> Canst thou not minister to a mind diseas'd,
> Pluck from the memory a rooted sorrow,
> Raze out the written troubles of the brain,
> And with some sweet oblivious antidote
> Cleanse the stuff'd bosom of that perilous stuff
> Which weighs upon the heart?

More remarkable are the examples of expanded metaphors; they are more natural than one would expect and greatly superior to the conceits in some of the history plays (*e.g. King John* IV. 1).

> *Duncan.* I have begun to *plant* thee and will labour
> To make thee full of *growing.*   Noble Banquo,
> That hast no less deserved, nor must be known
> No less to have done so, let me infold thee
> And hold thee to my heart.
>   *Banquo.*   There if I *grow,*
> The *harvest* is your own.
>   *Duncan.*   My *plenteous* joys
> *Wanton in fulness,* seek to hide themselves
> In drops of sorrow.

A more difficult combination and evolution is:

> his virtues
> Will plead like angels, trumpet-tongued against
> The deep damnation of his taking off;
> And pity, like a naked new-born babe,
> Striding the blast, or heaven's cherubin, hors'd
> Upon the sightless couriers of the air,
> Shall blow the horrid deed in every eye,
> That tears shall drown the wind.   I have no spur
> To prick the sides of my intent, but only
> Vaulting ambition, which o'erleaps itself
> And falls on the other.

Angels trumpet-tongued, the *naked new-born babe* and *heaven's cherubin* are associated, while *hors'd*, *couriers*, *spur to prick the sides*, *vaulting*, *o'erleaps* follow naturally. The thought is already in Shakespeare's head for at the close of scene 4 we have:

> The Prince of Cumberland!   That is a step
> On which I must fall down, or else o'erleap,
> For in my way it lies;

and in scene 6:

> We cours'd him at the heels, and had a purpose
> To be his purveyor; but he rides well,
> And his great love, sharp as his spur, hath holp him
> To his home before us.

After Lady Macbeth's entrance in our scene (7), Macbeth says:

> I have bought
> Golden opinions from all sorts of people,
> Which would be worn now in their newest gloss,
> Not cast aside so soon.

(The parallel with *Julius Caesar* has been noted.)   She replies:

> Was the hope drunk,
> Wherein you dress'd yourself?   Hath it slept since,
> And wakes it now, to look so green and pale?

This is very close to:

> O, where hath our intelligence been drunk,
> Where hath it slept?   (*King John*.)

But Lady Macbeth adds *dress'd*, taking it up from his *worn in their newest gloss*, and not content with that passes on to a new idea with *green and pale*.

Macbeth's soliloquy on the death of the queen is another example; and one may add—

> This avarice
> Sticks deeper, *grows* with more pernicious *root*
> Than *summer-seeming* lust, and it hath been
> The sword of our slain kings; yet do not fear;
> Scotland hath *foisons* to fill up your will,

and the powerful metaphorical writing of such a piece as

> Come, seeling night,
> Scarf up the pitiful eye of tender day
> And with thy bloody and invisible hand
> Cancel and tear to pieces that great bond
> That makes me pale.

Coriolanus and *Antony and Cleopatra* complete the tragedies and inaugurate the final style. In them the balance between the diction and the character is still preserved.

I select as peculiar features of the final style: first the practice of pausing after the ninth syllable and with a short conjunction or other monosyllable dovetailing two lines together:

> As if you were a god to punish, not
> A man of their infirmity.

> In thy hands clutched as many millions, in
> Thy lying tongue both numbers.

> That like an eagle in a dove-cote, I
> Flutter'd your Volscians in Corioli.

> By laying defects of judgment to me, but
> You patch'd up your excuses.

in his Armenia
And others of his conquered kingdoms, I
Demand the like.

Next to thyself and my young rover, he's
Apparent to my heart.

The gods throw stones of sulphur on me, if
The box I gave you was not thought by me
A precious thing.

this abject, which
Takes prisoner the wild motion of the eye.

One of her women lawyer to me, for
I yet not understand the case myself.

But if I were as wise as honest, then
My purpose would prove well.

Weigh'd between loathness and obedience, at
Which end o' the beam should bow.

There are innumerable examples of this; it substitutes
a new rhythm for the couplet and the line upon line
movement.   Three other quotations will serve to show
the nature of the new method:

The inevitable prosecution of
Disgrace and horror.

Not cowardly put off my helmet to
My countryman.

Thy father was the Duke of Milan and
A prince of power.

Sir, are not you my father?
Thy mother was a piece of virtue, and
She said thou wast my daughter.

This obvious and elementary fact about Shakespeare's later versification has been examined by every

commentator and been the subject of catalogues and treatises.   Nevertheless it cannot be passed over and taken for granted here.   Two things are to be remembered.   First, that his command of metre was such that he could use blank verse with more ease than prose, and experiment in syntax and arrangement of clauses without rattling his chains; secondly, it has not been pointed out that where the situation demands " high seriousness ", this running-on and these light endings are avoided, and the weightier movement and stronger monosyllables of the central style (Othello's " It is the cause, it is the cause, my soul ") are preferred. Read Cleopatra's—

> Give me my robe, put on my crown, I have
> Immortal longings in me.   Now no more,
> The juice of Egypt's grape shall moist this lip . . .,

or the great appeals of Volumnia in the fifth act or even Prospero's

> Ye elves of hills, brooks, standing lakes and groves,

(and in *The Tempest* the feminine ending has become very insidious) and one realises that Shakespeare, unlike his successors, did not abuse his new freedom, but, when occasion demanded, retained absolute control.   In harmony with this is his habit of restraining the diction no less than the metre in moments of climax.   Thus Shakespeare in *Coriolanus* transcribed from North the tragic simplicity of Volumnia's opening words; above all:

> Think with thyself
> How more unfortunate than all living women
> Are we come hither.

And in this same scene he twice gains his effect by
simple repetition instead of by metaphor or conceit:

> for how can we,
> Alas, how can we for our country pray,
> Whereto we are bound, together with thy victory,
> Whereto we are bound?

and

> Aufidius, though I cannot make true wars,
> I'll frame convenient peace.   Now, good Aufidius,
> Were you in my stead, would you have heard
> A mother less, or granted less, Aufidius?

This triple iteration of the name is in its way as moving
as the more famous appeal, " But yet the pity of it,
Iago! O Iago, the pity of it, Iago ".   Similarly for the
death speech of Antony he uses the simple narrative
of North, adding and repeating twice the words,
" I am dying, Egypt, dying ".

Secondly, I would emphasise in the final style
Shakespeare's love of writing for its own sake.   The
best single symptom of this is, I think, his use of the
paradoxical construction, usually for the superlative.
Thus in *Coriolanus*:

> Then let the pebbles on the hungry beach
> Fillip the stars; then let the mutinous winds
> Strike the proud cedars 'gainst the fiery sun,
> *Murd'ring impossibility, to make*
> *What cannot be, slight work.*

The Cydnus speech of Enobarbus is punctuated with
these epigrammatic points.   The wind " did seem to
glow the delicate cheeks and *what they undid did* ";
Antony, " for his ordinary pays his heart, for what

his eyes eat only ".   Cleopatra " makes defect perfection ", she

> makes hungry
> Where most she satisfies; for vilest things
> Become themselves in her, that the holy priests
> Bless her when she is riggish.

So also Marina " starves the ears she feeds and makes
them hungry, the more she gives them speech ".   Or
here are another similar pair:

> There would he anchor his aspect *and die*
> *With looking on his life,*

and

> Anger's my meat; I sup upon myself
> And so shall *starve with feeding.*

In *Cymbeline* Posthumus is:

> A man worth any woman, overbuys me
> Almost the sum he pays.

When Imogen (according to Iachimo's report) gave
the bracelet:

> Her pretty action did outsell the gift
> And yet enriched it too.

Cloten says:

> from every one
> The best she has and she of all compounded
> Outsells them all.

Prospero delivers Miranda in similar terms:

> Do not smile at me that I boast her off,
> For thou shalt find she will outstrip all praise
> And make it halt behind her.

Or take the conceit:

> I do extend him, Sir, within himself,
> Crush him together rather than unfold
> His measure duly.

Florizel's speech to Perdita beginning, " What you do still betters what is done ", is constructed on the same principle.   All these have something in common —a fanciful way of treating the superlative—and are significant in the final style.

Another proof of Shakespeare's preoccupation with style and style only at the end of his life is the return to the idealistic imagery of his own poems, the imagery of Marlowe and of Spenser and their two schools. Typical of Elizabethan poetry before 1600 are:

> Zenocrate, lovelier than the love of Jove,
> Brighter than is the silver Rhodope,
> Fairer than whitest snow on Scythian hills,

and

> The snow, which doth the top of Pindus strew,
> Did never whiter shew;
> Nor Jove himselfe, when he a swan would be,
> For love of Leda, whiter did appeare.

Shakespeare in his poems is prettier than Marlowe, closer to Spenser; his flowers are the tracery of frost on glass.   But in the last plays he recaptures the early poetic manner and infuses it with something of the rapture of Marlowe.

> Chaste as the icicle
> That's curdied by the frost from purest snow
> And hangs on Dian's temple

(a typical Shakespearian " accumulated superlative ",
of the same *genre* as those discussed above).

> Whose blush doth thaw the consecrated snow
> That lies on Dian's lap.

>   this hand
> As soft as dove's down, and as white as it,
> Or Ethiopian's tooth, or the fanned snow
> That's bolted by the northern blasts twice o'er.

We have again the pagan deities.   Shakespeare, unlike
Marlowe, seldom stakes everything on a single name;
they are " as plates dropped from his pocket ".   He
prefers to pile up his effect; in *Hamlet* for instance—

> See what a grace was seated on his brow;
> Hyperion's curls; the front of Jove himself;
> An eye like Mars to threaten and command,
> A station like the herald Mercury,
> New-lighted on a heaven-kissing hill,

and in *Cymbeline*—

> His feet Mercurial, his Martial thigh,
> The brawns of Hercules, but his Jovial face . . .

Shakespeare was never so seduced by the mythology
as his contemporaries, but in the last plays he comes
fresh to the ideal names as Marlowe did before him.

>   Her eyes as jewel-like
> And cased as richly; in pace another Juno.

>   clothed like a bride
> For the embracements even of Jove himself.

> Your laboursome and dainty trims, wherein
> You made great Juno angry.

> No shepherdess, but Flora
> Peering in April's front.

> for feature laming
> The shrine of Venus or straight-pight Minerva;
> Postures beyond brief nature.

> violets dim
> But sweeter than the lids of Juno's eyes
> Or Cytherea's breath; pale prime-roses
> That die unmarried ere they can behold
> Bright Phoebus in his strength.

> And golden Phoebus never be beheld
> Of eyes again so royal.

> Cytherea,
> How bravely thou becom'st thy bed! fresh lily,
> And whiter than the sheets!

This last quotation bears witness to a further point. The lily and the rose are the all-too-familiar images or symbols of Elizabethan poetry. But in Shakespeare's later work they are far less artificial than in the poems and early comedies and sonnets. Contrast the quotation above or this other from *Cymbeline*:

> O, sweetest, fairest lily!
> My brother wears thee not the one half so well
> As when thou grew'st thyself,

with

> A natural war of lilies and of roses,

or

> A lily pale with damask dye to grace her,

or

> Her lily hand her rosy cheek lay under,
> Cozening the pillow of a lawful kiss.

There is a change both of metre and of feeling.   Or contrast—

> A lily prison'd in a gaol of snow
> Or ivory in an alabaster band;
> So white a friend engirds so white a foe

with

> Yet I'll not shed her blood
> Nor scar that whiter skin of hers than snow
> And smooth as monumental alabaster.

Monumental is apt here; Desdemona lies upon the bed which is to be her altar, like a figure upon a tomb.
Again in *Othello* we have:

> When I have pluck'd the rose,
> I cannot give it vital growth again,
> It needs must wither; I'll smell it on the tree.

After *Hamlet* the rose almost disappears; this is a notable exception. We have a metaphorical use in *Antony and Cleopatra*:

> Against the blown rose may they stop their nose
> That kneeled unto the buds.

The images of *The Winter's Tale* and *Cymbeline*, then, flower naturally from an English soil; they have not the Italian grace of the blooms of *Venus and Adonis*.
Polixenes and Camillo discuss Perdita as follows:

> This is the prettiest low-born lass that ever
> Ran on the green-sord; nothing she does or seems
> But smacks of something greater than herself,
> Too noble for this place.
>   He tells her something
> That makes her blood look out.   Good sooth, she is
> The queen of curds and cream.

What a far remove from the *Epithalamium*:

> Her cheeks like apples which the sun hath rudded,
> Her lips like cherries charming men to bite,
> Her brest like to a bowl of cream uncrudded
> Her paps like lilies budded . . .

But it was in this school that Shakespeare first learnt the language of poetry.

To return for a moment to the pagan mythology, I am struck by another more general use which recurs in the final plays, for climax and conclusion.

> O mother, mother,
> What have you done?   Behold the heavens do ope,
> The gods look down, and this unnatural scene
> They laugh at. *(Coriolanus.)*

> Dissolve, thick cloud and rain, that I may say
> The gods themselves do weep.
> *(Antony and Cleopatra.)*

> This, this, no more, you gods, your present kindness
> Makes my past misery sport. *(Pericles.)*

> Laud we the gods
> And let our crooked smokes climb to their nostrils
> From our bless'd altars. *(Cymbeline.)*

> The blessed gods
> Purge all infection from the air whilst you
> Do climate here.
> You gods, look down
> And from your sacred vials pour your graces
> Upon my daughter's head. *(The Winter's Tale.)*

> Look down, you gods,
> And on this couple drop a blessed crown.
> *(The Tempest.)*

These last two provide a case of parallel passages which

are supposed by commentators to be almost unknown
in Shakespeare; add to them—

> The benediction of these covering heavens
> Fall on your heads like dew. (*Cymbeline.*)

All three are significant of a change of attitude in the
final comedies. It is curious with what persistency the
gods are invoked, although natural enough in the
classical plays. Also one must not forget the passing
of a statute in 1606 forbidding the taking of God's
name in vain upon the stage. In *Macbeth* we have
" God ", in *King Lear* " the gods "; and this small
point goes far towards distinguishing the " atmospheres "
of the two plays, and makes *Lear* the more Greek.

Next and perhaps most important of all in the final
style is the syntax. The chief characteristic of this is
the condensation, exemplified by a fondness for ellipsis,
inverted order, apposition, and parenthesis; with these
go speed of transition which is natural enough in
dialogue; here is a simple instance:

> O lady, weep no more, lest I give cause
> To be suspected of more tenderness
> Than doth become a man.   I will remain
> The loyal'st husband that did e'er plight troth.
> My residence in Rome at one Philario's,
> Who to my father was a friend, to me
> Known but by letter; thither write, my queen,
> And with mine eyes I'll drink the words you send,
> Though ink be made of gall. (*Cymbeline.*)

> I embrace you.
> Give me my robes, I am wild in my beholding.
> O! heavens, bless my girl.   But, hark! what music? (*Pericles.*)

Facts are often wedged in among poetic flourishes and speakers are in one line perfunctory, in the next leisurely and fanciful. In scenes where the story has to be lugged on its way, Shakespeare is like a peacock who picks his casual way and then quite suddenly unfurls the glory of his tail; sometimes there is only a glimpse, sometimes the full fan. In *Pericles* III. 3, we have such a scene; for instance—

> Till she be married, madam,
> By bright Diana, whom we honour, all
> Unscissar'd shall this hair of mine remain . . .
>
> We'll bring your grace e'en to the edge of the shore
> *Then give you up to the mask'd Neptune and*
> *The gentlest winds of heaven.*

or in *The Winter's Tale*, IV. 3, Camillo in the midst of his grave advice spreads poetic plumage—

> A course more promising
> Than a wild dedication of yourselves
> To unpath'd waters, undream'd shores.

Prospero suddenly remembering the conspiracy, breaks up the lovers' masque in a passion " that works him strongly "; yet he can soar into ten lines of undramatic and irrelevant, although unsurpassed, poetry. Very common are such little flourishes as Imogen's—

> ere I could
> Give him that parting kiss which I had set
> Betwixt two charming words, comes in my father,
> *And like the tyrannous breathing of the north*
> *Shakes all our buds from growing.*

Aristotle laid down the axiom:—τῇ δὲ λέξει δεῖ διαπονεῖν
ἐν τοῖς ἀργοῖς μέρεσιν καὶ μήτε ἠθικοῖς μήτε διανοητικοῖς.
ἀποκρύπτει γὰρ πάλιν ἡ λίαν λαμπρὰ λέξις τά τε ἤθη
καὶ τὰς διανοίας. And in the tragedies, from *Othello* to
Antony and Cleopatra, Shakespeare conforms to the
principle; but in the last plays he follows his fancy
and exploits his vocabulary.

Every speech provides instances of curious construction which make selection a difficult problem.
But here is a favourite arrangement of clauses:

> 'tis slander
> Whose edge is sharper than the sword, whose tongue
> Outvenoms all the worms of Nile, whose breath
> Rides on the posting winds and doth belie
> All corners of the world.   (*Cymbeline.*)

> 'tis wonder
> That an invisible instinct should frame them
> To royalty unlearn'd, honour untaught,
> Civility not seen from other, valour
> That wildly grows in them but yields a crop
> As if it had been sowed.   (*Cymbeline.*)

> The climate's delicate, the air most sweet,
> Fertile the isle, the temple much surpassing
> The common praise it bears.   (*Winter's Tale.*)

> This jealousy
> Is for a precious creature; as she's rare
> Must it be great, and, as his person's mighty,
> Must it be violent, and as he does conceive
> He is dishonour'd by a man which ever
> Profess'd to him, why his revenges must
> In that be made more bitter.   (*Winter's Tale.*)

>   I do not know
> One of my sex; no woman's face remember,
> Save, from my glass, mine own; nor have I seen
> More that I may call men than you, good friend,
> And my dear father; how features are abroad,
> I am skill-less of; but, by my modesty—
> The jewel in my dower—I would not wish
> Any companion in the world but you.   (*The Tempest.*)

Shakespeare's cumulative devices have been pointed out all through. The method illustrated above is a subtle consummation of the earlier uses. Instead of word upon word or line upon line, we have clause upon clause (often similar in meaning), arranged at cross currents with the metre; and in the clauses themselves the order of the words is sometimes inverted, the construction varied.

Condensation is gained by inserting numerous clauses which correspond to the ablative absolute construction in Latin, and participles, both present and past, are strung on to the main thread. With these go an ever-increasing fondness for parenthesis. Iachimo's confession exemplifies this well, which begins:

> Upon a time—unhappy was the clock
> That struck the hour—it was in Rome—accurs'd
> The mansion where—'twas at a feast—O would
> Our viands had been poison'd, or at least
> Those which I heav'd to head—the good Posthumus—
> What should I say? he was too good to be
> Where ill men were . . .

This is exceptional; and one must not forget that the Italian is shuffling and stammering and postponing the revelation. But Posthumus's speech in V. 3, describing the battle would serve to illustrate my point equally well, or Prospero's exposition in the second scene of *The Tempest*.

These characteristics of the final style invite an inquiry into the authorship of *The Two Noble Kinsmen*. Mr. Dugdale Sykes in the least convincing of his *Sidelights* ascribes the play to Massinger and Fletcher, and does not allow Shakespeare a line of it. If he is right, it will at least be admitted that in this play Massinger not only achieved poetic heights such as he never after approached, but also that he caught the very accent of the later Shakespeare at his best. I am not convinced by Mr. Sykes, although his essay makes one suspect Massinger of having had a third hand in the pie. Also it must be remembered that since Massinger was steeped in Shakespeare and fond of echoing his master, all evidence on stylistic grounds is rather two-edged. Thus Mr. Sykes notes a parallel passage at the beginning of I. 3, and claims that it is conclusive of Massinger's authorship; he adds, " Though he (Massinger) has many echoes and reminiscences of Shakespearian passages, he does not slavishly reproduce their very words and manner of phrasing ". How then does Mr. Sykes explain at the end of the preceding scene—

> Let th' event,
> That never-erring arbitrator, tell us
> When we know all ourselves;

which recalls in Troilus and Cressida—

> And that old common arbitrator time
> Will one day end it.

There are many weak points in Mr. Sykes's evidence, trifling in themselves which detract from his weightier arguments. For instance, he twice quotes parallel passages in which the sentiment is the same but the expression significantly different.
In I. 1:

> Extremity that sharpens sundry wits
> Makes me a fool.

In Massinger, *The Honest Man's Fortune*:

> . . . cunning calamity
> That others' gross wits uses to refine
> When I most need it dulls the edge of mine.

Again in I. 3:

> Though I know
> His ocean needs not my poor drops yet they
> Must lay their tribute here.

And in Massinger, *Believe as you List*:

> Though I know
> The ocean of your apprehensions needs not
> The rivulet of my poor cautions.

Both these parallels illustrate admirably the compactness and economy of Shakespeare's later style on which I have been insisting. The second is clearly a deliberate imitation with the metaphorical expansion typical of Massinger. And we may compare a similar metaphor twice employed in *The Comedy of Errors*; also in *Romeo and Juliet*:

> Back, foolish tears, back to your native spring,
> Your tributary drops belong to woe.

In the first parallel, the sentiment or *gnome* is one of

Q 2

those recurrent in the Elizabethan dramatists, while the expression, the matter-of-fact " makes me a fool ", the epithet " sundry ", the relegation of the metaphor into the one word " sharpens " are all Shakespearian.

It is damaging that Mr. Sykes selects to prove his case such everyday phrases as " levy our worthiest instruments ", " seal ", " dispatch this grand act of our life " (of a marriage). All of them are employed by any of the dramatists. *Seal* and *dispatch* occur innumerable times, and although Shakespeare does not have occasion to use the last phrase of a marriage, yet the word *act* with him is constantly used of lovers, " the act of sport ", " the act of darkness ", " to commit some loving act upon her ", and may have that significance here. Then elsewhere Mr. Sykes says that the word *deliver* in the sense of " describe ", " represent " is not found in Shakespeare. But in *Pericles*, Act V., we have:

> As my good nurse Lychorida hath oft
> Delivered weeping.

> I will believe you by the syllable
> Of what you shall deliver.

> Will you deliver
> How this dead queen relives,

and in *The Winter's Tale*, V. 1, " Heard the old shepherd deliver the manner how he found it ". There are other examples, but as the scene is a prose one and of no particular individuality, the point need not be laboured further.

Then Mr. Sykes argues that Massinger must have been capable of the fine line—

> Like to a pair of lions smeared with prey,

because he wrote—

> Like falcons on the stretch to seize the prey;

but this is no more conclusive than to quote—

> Like lions wanting food,
> Do rush upon us as their hungry prey,

or

> And to grin like lions
> Upon the pikes o' th' hunters.

There were more writers than one who could rise to that sort of thing.   But *smeared* is the significant word, and, Mr. Sykes omits to remark, one of which Shakespeare is fond:

> Triumphant death, smeared with captivity.

> Lo, now my glory smeared in dust and blood.

> This dread and black complexion smeared
> With heraldry more dismal.

> If any such be here—
> As it were sin to doubt—that love this painting
> Wherein you see me smeared.

> And smear with dust their glittering golden hours.

Then as a parallel to " Did I not . . . cure their surfeit that craves a present medicine ", Mr. Sykes quotes from Massinger:

> since the wound requires a sudden cure,

and

> the wound given to my daughter
> Which, in our leisure, you are bound to cure.

But in the *Two Noble Kinsmen* the metaphor is of a surfeit and not of a wound and (common enough in Shakespeare) has a far better parallel in *Othello*:

> My hopes, not surfeited to death
> Stand in bold cure.

But the idea is frequent in the Elizabethans.   In our play we have—

> I must no more believe thee on this point
> Than I will trust a sickly appetite
> That loathes even as it longs,

and Mr. Sykes quotes from *A Very Woman*—

> No more of love, good father,
> It was my surfeit and I loathe it now
> As men in fevers meat they fell sick on;

but why is this a better parallel than—

> your affections are
> A sick man's appetite who desires most that
> Which would increase his evil.   (*Coriolanus.*)

It is extraordinary that in III. 1, a scene of some hundred and thirty lines, peculiarly Shakespearian in merit and metre, Mr. Sykes only finds one parallel to quote:

> [thou] hast likewise blest a place
> With thy sole presence.

The fact that Massinger is fond of this expression is not sufficiently conclusive.   After all Shakespeare has " I am blest in your acquaintance ", " that he may bless the bay with his tall ship ", " that beauty am I bless'd with ". Besides, the lines must be read in their context:

> The duke has lost Hippolyta; each took
> A several land. This is a solemn rite
> They owe *bloom'd May*. *O queen Emilia,*
> *Fresher than May, sweeter*
> *Than her gold buttons on the boughs, or all*
> *Th' enamell'd knacks o' the mead or garden!* Yea,
> We challenge too the bank of any nymph,
> That makes the stream seem flowers; thou, O jewel,
> O' the wood, o' the world, hast likewise bless'd a place
> With thy sole presence! In thy rumination
> That I, poor man, might eftsoons come between,
> And *chop* on some cold thought! *thrice blessed chance*
> *To drop on such a mistress, expectation*
> *Most guiltless on't.* Tell me, O Lady Fortune—
> Next after Emily, my sovereign—how far
> I may be proud? . . .

In swiftness of transition, in movement (the strong mid-pauses and overflowing endings), in lyrical working, in verbal surprises (*knacks o' the mead, chop on some cold thought*) in use of parenthesis and ellipsis, this speech and the whole scene that follows it betray the ear and eye and mind of Shakespeare. The exclamations recall Perdita's " O Proserpina ", Iachimo's " Cytherea, how bravely thou becomest thy bed! ", Troilus's " Tell me, Apollo, for thy Daphne's love, what Cressid is . . ."

In the first act the Shakespearian imprint is far deeper than any traces of Massinger detected by Mr. Sykes. For instance, the development of metaphor in

ll. 106-111 exemplifies what I have already said in
connection with *Macbeth*.   At 122 we have:

> If that you were
> The ground-piece of some painter, I would buy you
> T' instruct me 'gainst a capital grief indeed.

A similar idea is in *Cymbeline*:

> One but painted thus
> Would be interpreted a thing perplexed
> Beyond self-explication.

We may compare the following in the same speech—

> Your sorrow beats so ardently upon me,
> That it shall make a counter-reflect 'gainst
> My brother's heart and warm it to some pity
> Though it were made of stone,

with two passages in *Troilus and Cressida*:

> His virtues shining upon others
> Heat them, and they retort that heat again
> To the first giver,

and

> Or like a gate of steel,
> Fronting the sun, receives and renders back
> His figure and his heat.

The First Queen's speech, l. 131, is Shakespearian in
rhythm and construction, and

> O Jove, your actions
> Soon as they move, as osprayes do the fish,
> Subdue before they touch,

recalls in *Coriolanus*, IV. 7. 32:

> I think he'll be to Rome
> As is the osprey to the fish, who takes it
> By sovereignty of nature.

Certain words also should be noted: uncandied, warranting moonlight, blubbered queens, budge, un-panged judgment—this last particularly. (In *Cymbeline* we have " Thy memory will then be pang'd by me ".) Shakespeare likes to form adjectives on this principle: cp. unrough, unpolicied, unking'd, unqualified.

In I. 3 Pirithous says to Emilia:

> My precious maid,
> Those best affections that the heavens infuse [1]
> In their best tempered pieces, keep enthroned
> In your dear heart.

This blessing strongly recalls those of Gonzalo, Leontes, Belarius, Hermione, Prospero.

In I. 4 we have the rare metaphor:

> The very lees of such, millions of rates
> Exceed the wine of others;

which is found in *Macbeth*:

> The wine of life is drawn and the mere lees
> Is left this vault to brag of.

With III. 1 I have already dealt. In the last act Shakespeare emerges at moments and shows his back above the ooze, but the writing is very uneven and some of the invocations are pretentious instead of sublime. Part, however, of Arcite's speech to Mars (49-68) is as fine as anything in *The Tempest* and very reminiscent of that play in rhythm and language; but I doubt whether Shakespeare touched anything else in this scene. There are glimmerings of him in scenes

---

[1] Cp. " Infused with a fortitude from heaven." (*The Tempest*.)

3 and 4; for instance, one of the favourite paradoxes already noted:

> To buy you I have lost what's dearest to me,
> Save what is bought; and yet I purchase cheaply,
> As I do rate your value.

Characteristic in the Shakespearian portions of the play is the combination of complexity of thought and compactness of style, which sometimes leads to obscurity, as in—

> How his longing
> Follows his friend! since his depart, his sports,
> Though craving seriousness and skill, pass'd slightly
> His careless execution, where nor gain
> Made him regard, or loss consider: but
> Playing one business in his hand, another
> Directing in his head, his mind nurse equal
> To these so differing twins;

and

> Were they metamorphos'd
> Both into one—O, why? there were no woman
> Worth so compos'd a man; their single share
> Their nobleness peculiar to them, gives
> The prejudice of disparity, values shortness
> To any lady breathing.

But above all it is in rhythm, in construction and in language, in the use of parenthesis and apposition of vigorous monosyllables and original epithets that we detect the author of *Cymbeline* and *The Winter's Tale*.

Before leaving Shakespeare's final style we may note that in one respect *Antony and Cleopatra* stands out among the other plays; namely, in richness of symbolical writing; for example:

> Alack, our terrene moon
> Is now eclips'd; and it portends alone
> The fall of Antony;

and Antony's speech to Eros on the signs that are black vesper's pageant, which has a parallel in *The Tempest*.   Then in the monument scene, Cleopatra's—

> O sun,
> Burn the great sphere thou mov'st in; darkling stand
> The varying star o' the world,

and

> The crown o' the earth doth melt.   My lord!
> O wither'd is the garland of the war,
> The soldier's pole is fall'n; young boys and girls
> Are level now with men.   The odds is gone,
> And there is nothing left remarkable
> Beneath the visiting moon.

and in the last scene the cry of Iras—

> Finish, good lady; the bright day is done,
> And we are for the dark.

VII

CONCLUSIONS AND SOME FURTHER COMMENTS

THE CHARACTERISTICS and the development of the Shakespearian style have now been pursued from the opening to the close of his dramatic career. Among other things I have particularly emphasised the important part played by his prose, and the Latinising of his vocabulary. I have touched, as an amateur, upon one or two points of versification, and noted changes of rhythm and construction. Above all, the concrete element in his diction, or rather the combinations of concrete and abstract words, cannot be made too much of; nor can I resist examining this a little more minutely.

The hendiadys uses of *Hamlet* have been considered, also the pairing of epithets. Then the telling effect of a word which " grazes vulgarity " is well known (to all except Dr. Johnson). For instance Hamlet's

> Exposing what is mortal and unsure
> To all that fortune, death and danger dare,
> Even for an egg-shell,

and Aufidius

> Breaking his oath and resolution like
> A twist of rotten silk.

The colloquial element is absolutely essential in verse drama. But in Shakespeare we have some other remarkable practices. In the earlier plays he makes not a little play with " physical words ".

Thus in *Titus Andronicus*, " The ragged entrails of the pit ", " The brinish bowels of the surge ", which is better than " the fatal bowels of the deep " in *Richard III*. In *Henry VI*.:

> A viperous worm
> That gnaws the bowels of the commonwealth.

In *Richard II*.:

> Gaunt as a grave
> Whose hollow womb inherits nought but death.

In *Henry V*.:

> Through the foul womb of night
> The hum of either army stilly sounds.

In *Romeo and Juliet*:

> Thou detestable maw, thou womb of death,
> Thus I enforce thy rotten jaws to open.

In *A Midsummer Night's Dream*:

> The jaws of darkness do devour it up.

In *Richard III*.:

> So, now prosperity begins to mellow
> And drop into the rotten mouth of death;

and in *King John*:

> Ye bloody Neroes ripping up the womb
> Of your dear mother England.

Lear and Timon in their curses speak the same physical language (which is characteristic of the school of Kyd) but with a difference. And they are more pitiless. Milton in his lines on Time imitates the Elizabethans:

> And glut thyself with what thy womb devours.

But as Shakespeare advanced the possibilities of metaphor became more subtle and by a kind of personification he succeeded in persuading his style to carry a large proportion of abstract words.   His habit is to couple his abstract nouns with a vivid verb, usually one denoting human action.   For example, the following: " Expectation fainted, longing for what it had not "; " Emulation hath a thousand sons that one by one pursue "; " A deed whereat valour would weep"; " the expedition of my violent love outrun the pauser, reason "; " thriftless ambition that will ravin up thy own life's means "; " Sluttery to such neat excellence oppos'd, Should make desire vomit emptiness "; " admiration did not hoop at them "; " makes antiquity for aye his page ";

> injury of chance
> Puts back leave-taking, jostles roughly by
> All time of pause, rudely beguiles our lips
> Of all rejoindure, forcibly prevents
> Our lock'd embrasures, strangles our dear vows. . . .

To this usage we may add such a phrase as " Bring in the admiration " and Prospero's address to Caliban— " Shrugg'st thou, malice ", and to Ariel—" Bravely, my diligence ".   On the other hand, there are the personifications: " That smooth-faced Gentleman, tickling Commodity ", " the false housewife Fortune ", " that old common arbitrator Time ", etc.   The personifications of the eighteenth-century poets are created in marble or in paint, those of Shakespeare in flesh and blood, or rather in character.[1]

---

[1] Coleridge remarked the use of the word " flatter " in

> " Full many a glorious morning have I seen
> Flatter the mountain tops with sovereign eye ",

an example of Shakespeare's practice similar to those quoted above.   Cp. p. 201.

One small point which is worth mentioning is Shakespeare's tendency to repeat a word or image, rather weakly, in the same play.   In his early work, this comes, I think, from poverty of language and ideas, but in his later work from speed.   For instance, in *Two Gentlemen of Verona*, Proteus says:

> My love is thawed,
> Which like a waxen image 'gainst the fire
> Bears no impression of the thing it was.

Only a few scenes later the Duke says:

> This weak impress of love is as a figure
> Trenched in ice, which with an hour's heat
> Dissolves to water and doth lose his form.

It is the image Shakespeare uses at this time, afterwards substituting "discandy" and "melting sweets". In *Venus and Adonis*:

> What wax so frozen but dissolves with tempering,
> And yields at last to every light impression?

In *King John*:

> even as a form of wax
> Resolveth from his figure 'gainst the fire.

In *Midsummer Night's Dream*:

> To whom you are but as a form of wax
> By him imprinted and within his power
> To leave the figure or disfigure it.

An even closer repetition comes in *Richard II*. Mowbray says:

> And now my tongue's use is to me no more
> Than an unstringed viol or a harp.

Only two scenes after, Northumberland speaks of John of Gaunt's death:

> His tongue is now a stringless instrument.

In *Richard III*. Shakespeare seems to be taken by the word *dally*.

> Our aery buildeth in the cedars' top
> And dallies with the wind and scorns the sun.

> Take heed you dally not before your king.

> Not dallying with a brace of courtesans.

> That high All-seer which I dallied with.

Stanley's

> Farewell; the leisure and the fearful time
> Cuts off the ceremonious vows of love,

is poorly echoed by Richmond:

> More than I have said, loving countrymen,
> The leisure and enforcement of the time
> Forbids to dwell on.

In *Romeo and Juliet*, III. 2. 99:

> Ah, poor my lord, what tongue shall smooth thy name
> When I thy three hours' wife have mangled it.

Only ninety lines later, in a different context:

> How hast thou the heart
> To mangle me with that word " banished ".

In *The Comedy of Errors*,

> as easy mayst thou fall
> A drop of water in the breaking gulf,
> And take unmingled thence that drop again,
> Without addition or diminishing,
> As take from me thyself and not me too,

is anticipated two scenes before by—

> I to the world am like a drop of water,
> That in the ocean seeks another drop,
> Who failing there to find his fellow forth,
> Unseen, inquisitive, confounds himself.

A simile in the first ten lines of *A Midsummer Night's Dream* surprises us:

> This old moon wanes; she lingers my desires
> Like to a step-dame or a dowager
> Long withering out a young man's revenue.

Thus Theseus to Hippolyta. After their exit, in the same scene, Lysander says to Hermia:

> I have a widow aunt, a dowager
> Of great revenue, and she hath no child.

The dowager was part of the story, and whatever Shakespeare happened to have in his head, he turned into his verse, without going farther afield. *Dowager* only once occurs elsewhere, and then in *Henry VIII.* In *Antony and Cleopatra* we have the memorable passage, "the maid that milks and does the meanest chares". Two scenes later:

> And when thou hast done this chare, I'll give thee leave
> To play till doomsday.

The word is not found elsewhere in Shakespeare. "Discandy," also, in the same play is used twice, and in no other play. Again, in *Troilus and Cressida*, one is struck by Shakespeare's sudden fondness for *emulous* and *emulation*. Both occur four times and the first is

not otherwise used.   Mr. Middleton Murry, in an
essay on *Coriolanus*, makes a good deal of the passage—

> O, let me clip ye
> In arms as sound as when I woo'd, in heart
> As merry as when our nuptial day was done,
> And tapers burn'd to bedward.

He is occupied with that retiring figure Virgilia and
intends that this word with which Marcius greets
Cominius should redound indirectly to her credit.
But Mr. Murry has not remarked that Aufidius reconciles himself to Coriolanus in exactly the same way.

> Know thou first,
> I lov'd the maid I married; never man
> Sigh'd truer breath; but that I see thee here,
> Thou noble thing, more dances my rapt heart
> Than when I first my wedded mistress saw
> Bestride my threshold.

Not a few of the similes of the early plays reappear in a
condensed form many years after, more symbolical or
more effective.   Thus the Bastard—

> Your sword is bright, sir, put it up again,

becomes on Othello's lips—

> Put up your bright swords, or the dew will rust them.

Charmian's " Downy windows, close ", is in Richard
III. less poetically—

> Ere I let fall the windows of my eyes.

John of Gaunt's

> My oil-dried lamp and time-bewasted light
> Shall be extinct with age and endless night,
> My inch of taper shall be burnt and done,

and Clifford's

> Here burns my candle out; ay, here it dies
> Which while it lasted gave King Henry light,

becomes Macbeth's " Out, out, brief candle ".

Then like the other poets Shakespeare has his favourite adjectives which recur. I am particularly conscious of two: *rich* and *envious*. The first has various extended uses:—*rich conceit, rich music, rich blood, rich opinion, rich golden shaft, rich wisdom, rich thievery, richest eyes, rich honesty,*

> The rich advantage of good exercise.
> . . . doth think it rich
> To hear the wooden dialogue. . . .

Keats also is Shakespearian in his fondness for it. Open Rupert Brooke's 1914, and you will find—

> Blow out, you bugles, over the rich Dead,

and

> . . . lit by the rich skies all day,

and

> In that rich earth a richer dust concealed,

and

> as a mother who
> Has watched her children all the rich day through.

Like Milton before him, he robbed the Elizabethans and " cramm'd his rich thievery up, he knows not how ".

Envious Shakespeare lingers over. He applies it to the forces of nature. " Each envious briar his weary legs doth scratch ", " the envious clouds ", " what envious streaks do lace the severing clouds in yonder

East ", " the envious siege of watery Neptune ", " the sea whose envious gulf did swallow up his life ", " some envious surge will in his brinish bowels swallow him ", " still the envious flood kept in my soul ", " like envious floods o'errun her lovely face ", " an envious sneaping frost ", " the bud bit by an envious worm ", " envious and calumniating Time ". Others besides myself must, I imagine, have been struck by these passages and by the dramatic effectiveness of putting human puppets at the mercy of nature and endowing fate with one of the deadly sins. " Can heaven be so envious? " cries Juliet, and Cressida echoes her, " Have the gods envy? Ay, ay, ay, it is too plain a case." One thinks of Thomas Hardy. Milton in his Elizabethan lines borrows the same epithet, " Fly, envious Time ".

Notes and Quotations need no peroration. I have marshalled together here my private reflections and discoveries. Their importance lies in the angle from which the subject is attacked. My plea is that readers of Shakespeare should focus their eyes more sharply upon the matter in hand and exchange wonder for curiosity.

THE END